Joyful Goo
for
Young and Old

Victor Galeone

Magnificat Institute Press
Houston
2014

First Edition, 2014 by Magnificat Institute Press, P.O. Box 60591, Houston, TX 77205.

Book cover artwork is a copy of a painting for the Masthead of the Coming Home Network www.chnetwork.org. Used with permission.

Scripture quotations are translations or paraphrases by the author.

The artwork at the head the chapters identified by Virginia Broderick was obtained from Tarrywood Designs, Inc., P O Box 81, Bristol, CT 06011. Phone: (860) 583-3239, Used with permission.

All other permissions for excerpts or artwork used are documented in the corresponding endnotes at the back of the book.

Every effort has been made to determine copyright holders of excerpted materials and to secure permissions as needed. If any copyrighted materials have been inadvertently used in this work without proper credit given in one form or another, please notify Magnificat Institute Press in writing. Published 2014

Cover design by Sallie Saltzman at saltzmandesign.com

Printed in the United States of America.
ISBN 978-0-9657125-7-6
Library of Congress Card Catalog Number: 2014946017

References are found in the Endnotes after the Epilogue.

To all those—young and old alike—
who feel a frustrating void deep in their hearts.

May that God-shaped void be filled
with the love of Jesus, the source of all our joy!

Acknowledgements

Gerard B. Tall, Jr.

Nancy Ellis

Joe Difato

Rev. Michael Morgan, J.D., J.C.L.

Thomas Umlauf

Brother Anthony Maria

Abbot Stanislaus Gumula, O.C.S.O.

CONTENTS

INTRODUCTION

The following reflection, *One Solitary Life*, may be familiar to you. If so, please read it again—but this time, slowly and thoughtfully:

Here is a young man, the child of a peasant woman.
He was born in an obscure village, and grew up in another village,
    where he worked in a carpenter shop until he was thirty.
Then for three years he became a wandering preacher.
He never went to college. He never held an office.
He never had a family. He never led an army.
He never traveled two hundred miles from the place of his birth.
He did none of the things that usually accompany greatness.
He had no credentials but himself.
While still a young man,
    the tide of public opinion turned against him.
His friends ran away. One of them denied him.
Another turned him traitor. He went through the mockery of a trial.
He was nailed to a cross between two thieves.
While he was dying, his executioners gambled
    for the only thing he owned on this earth—his clothing.
When he was dead, he was laid in a borrowed grave
    through the pity of a friend.
Twenty centuries wide have come and gone,
    and today he is the central figure of the human race
    and the leader of the column of progress.
I am far within the mark when I say that all the armies that ever marched, and all the navies that ever sailed, and all the parliaments that ever sat, and all the kings that ever reigned—put together—have not affected the life of man upon this earth as much as that
                    One Solitary Life.
                    —Anonymous, late 1800s

Many people consider the preceding tribute to Jesus to be a gross exaggeration. But those who do so should realize that every single human being who ever walked our earth is stamped with the birth year of a crucified Galilean Jew: BC or AD.

BC = Before Christ / **AD** = A*nno Domini* (Year of Our Lord). While some groups do have their own systems for dating events—e.g. Jews, from the creation of the world, and Muslims, from the call of Mohammad, etc—but for validity, all their official documents must also contain the actual "AD year" in parentheses.

No certified document is valid without referring to the year when Jesus was born. Contracts, passports, birth certificates, etc—must all contain the date of the year they were issued: 1935, 1967, 2014—that is, two thousand and fourteen years since the birth of Jesus.

Some years ago I made a modest donation to a charitable group via a personal check. In a few days, my check was returned with a note: "Fill in the date. Check is non-negotiable without a date." In writing a check, a person acknowledges—unwittingly—that Jesus is the central figure of human history.

You are about to embark on a journey—a journey to look at Jesus in a new way. While he may be the central figure of human history, in reality, he wants to be the central figure of every human heart.

The human heart was made for joy, not for sadness. It withers when confronted with sorrow; it expands when bathed in joy. Jesus came to flood our hearts with that joy that we all crave. This is the message of Pope Francis's Apostolic Letter, *The Joy of the Gospel*, as well.

In the mid-1980s Mother Teresa opened an AIDS hospice in Washington DC, staffed by her Sisters. At the hospice some years ago, a man dying of AIDS requested to be baptized. When the priest asked him for an expression of faith, the dying man whispered: "All I know is that I'm miserable, and these Sisters are always happy—even when I curse them. Yesterday, I asked one of them why she was so happy. She answered, 'Jesus.' Well I want this Jesus, so that I can be happy too."

In closing, I will cite an anecdote concerning the late Cardinal Avery Dulles, the son of President Eisenhower's Secretary of State. While studying law at Harvard, the young Dulles became an agnostic. But as he walked along the Charles River one afternoon, the beauty of the spring blossoms and the serenading birds so moved him that he realized that the beauty and purpose in nature was meaningless without an all-powerful God. He later became a Catholic, and then went on to be ordained a Jesuit priest.

While he was teaching theology at the Catholic University during the 1960s, one day a student asked him, "Father Dulles, what would you consider to be the most important event of your career?"

Without a pause, Dulles responded, "The most important thing about my career…is the discovery of the pearl of great price, the treasure hidden in the field—the Lord Jesus himself."

This book was written to help everyone, young and old—but especially Catholic youth and young adults who no longer practice their faith, to experience the joy of discovering that "treasure hidden in the field."

1. Can I Be Sure That God Exists?

Al: Jo, why don't you believe in God?

Jo: Because I don't believe in the Bible.

Al: You don't need the Bible to show that God exists. You just have to use your head.

Jo: Nonsense!

Al: Let's say that we're walking along the seashore with not a soul in sight. Scrawled in the sand we see the words, "John loves Sally." I remark, "Hey, look what a seagull did!" Would you buy that?

Jo: Of course not!

Al: Then maybe it was the wind or the waves.

Jo: Impossible!

Al: Well, who put it there? No one's around.

Jo: Maybe someone who was there earlier—perhaps a jogger.

Al: Right on! An intelligible message requires an intelligent source.

Jo: Absolutely!

Al: Let's apply that to the human cell. There's more information in a single human cell than in all 30 volumes of the *Encyclopedia Britannica.* Well, how did all that information get there?

Jo: It just accumulated over eons of time.

Al: Blind chance cannot produce an intelligible message. What if you saw these letters on a Scrabble board, NDZKAWJXDE?

Jo: I'd say that someone drew those letters at random.

11

Al: Is that true of TOBEORNOTTOBETHATISTHEQUESTION?

Jo: No. They were deliberately arranged.

Al: True! So if inanimate forces like the wind and the waves cannot form three simple words in the sand, how much less can blind chance encode all the DNA information in every single living cell!

Jo: Just a minute! Snowflakes are produced by chance, and no two snowflakes are ever alike.

Al: That's true! Snowflakes are what scientists classify as patterns, which occur naturally with no help from a designer. But codes do not occur without an intelligent designer. Examples of codes include music and languages—like English—computer programs, and yes, DNA. Our minds will not rest until we admit that an Intelligent Designer is responsible for all that DNA information.

Jo: Well, if there is a God, how can he tolerate so much evil and suffering in the world?

Al: We'll get to that. But first, I want to ask some questions from general science. The moon is 240,000 miles distant from earth. What would happen if it were 50,000 miles closer?

Jo: There would be daily tsunamis and tidal waves everywhere.

Al: And what would the earth be like if there was considerably more oxygen in the atmosphere?

Jo: We'd have countless forest fires throughout the globe.

Al: And if the oxygen were a great deal less?

Jo: The advanced animals—like human beings—could not survive.

Al: Have you ever wondered why water is practically the only exception to the rule of the expansion and contraction of matter?

Jo: I don't follow you.

Al: In nature, most substances expand when heated and *contract* when cooled, except for water. From 100° to 4° Celsius, water—like all other substances—contracts. But from 4° to 0° water reverses itself and starts to expand again, causing the ice to float.

But if water kept on contracting as it approached 0°, ice would form on the bottom, due to its heavier density. How would that affect the lakes, ponds, and rivers up North during the winter?

Jo: They'd freeze solid from the bottom up—since there would be no insulating icecap on top to keep the water below from freezing.

Al: Exactly—destroying all the marine life in the process! Jo, do you think that all these examples I've been citing happened by mere chance?

Jo: I see where you're going, but I don't buy it. It's a scientific fact that all species evolved on their own through natural selection.

Al: Evolution—that is, macro-evolution—is not a fact but a theory, and a *weak* one at that! For a species to evolve from lower forms, there should be countless intermediate stages. But the fossil record is blank. No missing links have ever been found.

Jo: What about the Piltdown man?

Al: After being duped for 40 years, the British Museum of Natural History reported that the Piltdown man was the biggest hoax in the history of paleontology (the study of fossils).

Jo: Well, you still haven't explained why God allows so much evil in the world.

Al: In saying there's evil in the world, aren't you assuming that there's such a thing as good?

Jo: Yes, of course.

Al: How do you tell the difference between the two?

Jo: The same way I distinguish between red and green.

Al: Just a moment! You tell the difference between red and green by seeing, don't you?

Jo: Of course.

Al: But you can't *see* good and evil, can you? So again, how do you tell them apart?

Jo: On the basis of feeling; how else?

Al: In some cultures, they love their neighbors; in others, they eat them—both on the basis of feeling. Do you have a preference?

Jo: Hmm. I get your point.

Al: So by admitting there's evil in the world, don't you have to admit there's also good? And in admitting that there's good, don't you have to admit a moral law to distinguish good from evil?[1]

Jo: I suppose so.

Al: And by acknowledging a moral law, don't you also have to admit a Moral Lawgiver?

13

Jo: Why would a Moral Lawgiver permit evil?

Al: Because he gave us free will—the power to choose. In so doing, he took the risk that we might reject him by choosing what's evil.

Jo: Why would he have done that?

Al: Because God doesn't want robots or slaves. He wants us to freely choose to love him. That's the tragedy of our first parents

Jo: So you want me to buy all that nonsense about Adam and Eve and original sin, do you?

Al: You don't need the Bible to prove original sin, Jo. You only have to check the daily newspaper!

Jo: You mean about wars, murders and other gruesome crimes?

Al: Exactly! And that forces us to conclude: Something is radically wrong in human nature. We trace that radical evil back to our first parents. In order to have them prove their love, God put them to a test—a test they failed. *They* wanted to decide what was right or wrong. As a result, we all inherited their rebellion.

Jo: That seems so unfair.

Al: Not any more unfair than if you had a grandfather, who greedily squandered the family inheritance on risky, senseless gambling. What did he have to pass on to you, his descendant?

Jo: Not a penny.

Al: You're right. He blew it all through greed. And that's just about what original sin is like: It's the loss of God's friendship in our lives—something we had no right to. But God did not leave us orphans. He promised to send us a Savior—someone to make amends for all the evil in the world.
And that's what we'll be examining in our future discussions.

From Atheist to Catholic

Jennifer Fulwiler "always thought it was obvious that God did not exist." She grew up a content atheist. Having a profound respect for knowledge, particularly scientific knowledge, she was convinced that religion and reason were incompatible. Not surprisingly, she was also emphatically anti-Christian and, especially, anti-Catholic. "Catholic beliefs seemed bizarre and weird," she says.

Fulwiler would have been astonished to know that she and Joe Fulwiler, her husband, would come to embrace those "bizarre," "weird" beliefs. On Easter 2007, they entered the Catholic Church with deep joy and a sense of coming home!

Nona Aguilar, a correspondent for the *National Catholic Register*, interviewed Jennifer Fulwiler about her unexpected journey:

There is always a first step that leads to belief in God. What was yours?

Thanks to meeting and knowing my husband, I learned that belief in God is not fundamentally unreasonable. We met at the high-tech company where we both worked. Joe believed in God—something that, fortunately, I didn't know for a while.

Why was that fortunate?

To me, belief in God was so unreasonable that, by definition, no reasonable person could believe in such a thing! Had I known that Joe believed in God, I would never have dated him.

What was your reaction when you found out?

It gave me pause. Joe is too smart—brilliant, really, with degrees from Yale, Columbia and Stanford—to believe in something nonsensical. I also met many of his friends. They, too, are highly intelligent—some with MDs and PhDs from schools like Harvard and Princeton—and believed.

What caused you to consider the question more seriously?

I have always been a truth-seeker, which is why I was an atheist. But I had a prideful, arrogant way of approaching questions about life and meaning. I now realize that pride is the most effective way to block out God so that one doesn't see him at all. Certainly, I didn't.

The birth of our first child motivated me to seek the truth with humility. I can't emphasize this point enough: Humility, true humility is crucial to the conversion process.

Was your husband a help in this process?

Eventually, but not at first. Religion wasn't something we talked about. Joe was a non-churchgoing Baptist, which was fine by me. In fact, since I was an atheist, I considered not talking about God to be a good compromise. Our lives were completely secular—just like our wedding.

Was there ever an Aha! moment that finally made you abandon atheism?

Several, but one in particular actually shocked me. I asked myself two questions: What is information? And: Can information ever come from a non-intelligent source?

15

It was a shocking moment for me because I had to confront the fact that DNA is information. If I remained an atheist, I would have to believe that all the intricate, detailed, complex information contained in DNA comes out of nowhere and nothing. But I also knew that idea did not make sense. After all, I don't look at billboards—which contain much simpler information than DNA—and think that wind and erosion created them. That wouldn't be rational. Suddenly, I found that I was a very discomfited atheist.

Is that the point at which you began to believe in God?

No. But now I was a reluctant atheist. I had lots of questions but knew no one who might have answers. So, coming from the high-tech world, where did I go for answers? I put up a blog, of course! I started posting tough questions on my blog.

One matter stood out from the beginning: The best, most thoughtful responses came from Catholics. Incidentally, their answers were consistently better than the ones from atheists. It intrigued me that Catholics could handle anything I threw at them. Also, their responses reflected such an eminently reasonable worldview that I kept asking myself: How is it that Catholics have so much of this all figured out?

Was your husband helpful to you at this point?

As I started telling Joe some of the answers that I was getting, especially from Catholics, his own interest in religion—and Catholicism—was piqued. We have always been a great team, so it was wonderful that we were exploring the issues and questions together, especially since we were so anti-Catholic.

Both of you?

Yes. I thought the Church's views on most things, but especially marriage, contraception and abortion (since I was then ardently pro-choice), were simply crazy. Joe's anti-Catholicism, while different, was stronger and more settled. He didn't understand any Catholic doctrine or apologetics, so he fell into a stereotyped view of Catholics, thinking that they made idols of the pope and Mary, etc.[2]

There seems to be an uncanny similarity between Judeo-Christian theology and the new information theory, like DNA:

And God **said**, "Let there be light...." (Gn 1 & ff.)

"The heavens were made by the **word** of the Lord...
The Lord **spoke**, and the world came to be..." (Ps 33:6, 9)

"In the beginning was the **Word**...
through him all things were made." (Jn 1:1-3)

---

2. Why Am I Here...Where Am I Headed?

Al: Jo, now that we've seen how the world has no explanation without an Intelligent Designer—namely, God—could you tell me what life is all about? In other words, why are we here?

Jo: Why are we here? Just to live, enjoy life, and die.

Al: That's all? Well, let's say that tonight you retire in your own bed as usual. Then pretend that you wake up to find yourself on a train traveling at full speed in a compartment with four strangers. How would you react?

Jo: The first thing I'd want to know is how I got there. And secondly, where the train was headed.

Al: Your fellow travelers respond amid jovial smiles: "Who cares? Sit back, relax and enjoy the scenery out there." Well, could you?

Jo: Of course not! How can you relax during a nightmare?

Al: Precisely! Yet that's how countless people spend their entire lives. They have no idea where they came from, where they're heading, or even why they exist. And they could care less.

Jo: Hmmm. How do you resolve that dilemma?

Al: By discovering the answer to those basic questions. First of all, how did we get here?

Jo: From our parents.

Al: That's right. And they came from their parents and we go back all the way to the very first parents at the beginning of time. And where did the first couple come from?

Jo: Well, as we discussed last time, from the Intelligent Designer.

17

Al: Exactly! God created us human beings as the peak of the whole material world—even above the animal kingdom. Do you know what makes us different from brute animals?

Jo: I've never given that a thought.

Al: Animals operate on instinct, but we don't. A horse can no more go on a hunger strike than a dog can control himself when the female is in heat. That's why animals, driven by nature, are not accountable for their actions.

Jo: But isn't that the same with us?

Al: Not at all. Since we have free will, we're responsible for what we do. That's why a man forcing a woman to have sex is guilty of rape. So given the choice between good and evil, we should always choose what's good. That's how we fulfill life's purpose.

Jo: Which is?

Al: Happiness! God wants us to be happy—that's why he made us.

Jo: I don't see it that way—not with all the suffering in the world.

Al: We'll visit that later. First, let's examine some revealing items. We need nourishment to survive. A major source of food are the carbohydrates—a compound of carbon. Do you agree?

Jo: What's that got to do with happiness?

Al: Simply this: Carbon is also the main component of gasoline. So if God had designed our stomachs differently—like the engine of a car—then instead of having a mouth-watering pizza for lunch, we might be downing a pint of "Regular." But no! Our digestive system is designed to nourish us, while at the same time giving us pleasure—thereby contributing to our happiness.

Jo: That's a mere coincidence.

Al: Really? Is our reproductive system also a mere coincidence? Mind you, God could have designed it like that of the plants.

Jo: Get serious—please!

Al: I am serious. God is all-powerful. Instead of having us multiply by means of the love embrace between husband and wife—with all its joy and pleasure—he could have designed us to reproduce like the flowers, which deliver pollen from the male stamens to the female pistil (ovary). In that case, the husband might fertilize his wife with a mere sneeze—without even having to touch her. But no—God wanted it to be a joyful occasion for us.

Jo: Are you saying that whatever we do in life implies that we're searching for happiness?

Al: Absolutely!

Jo: Even the fellow who blows his brains out?

Al: Yes, even him! He's so miserable that he figures: "If there is anything beyond the grave, it can't be as bad as the misery I'm now experiencing. So I might as well end it all."

Jo: Hmm. I just saw where the teenage suicide rate has increased 5,000 percent since 1950! Unreal!

Al: And it will only get worse unless our teens learn what the real meaning of life is.

Jo: I'm confused. Why would God give us free will at the risk of having us reject him?

Al: Because as we discussed the last time, God wants us to love him freely—a thing that robots and brute animals cannot do. A love that's forced is not love—period!

Jo: So just what is the ultimate goal that will satisfy the longing that we all have for happiness?

Al: That's an excellent question. We've all been created with a God-shaped void in our hearts that only God can fill. It's tragic how most folks go through life without ever realizing it.

Jo: If it's so fundamental, how can they not realize it? You mean to say that they're clueless?

Al: Oh no! They replace the Creator with a creature. They try to force wealth or power or pleasure into that God-shaped hole—hoping it will satisfy them. As Chesterton once observed: "Every man knocking on the door of a brothel is searching for God."

Jo: Then a creature can't completely satisfy us.

Al: That's right! After the experience is over, a God-substitute only makes us more miserable than we were before. As Augustine, an early Christian writer, said: "You have formed us for yourself, O Lord—and our hearts are restless until they rest in you."

Jo: Well, as a Christian, he's only preaching the party line.

Al: Ah, but Bertrand Russell, an avowed atheist, said something quite similar: "Unless you assume [there's] a God, the question of life's purpose is meaningless."

Jo: He's got a point there. So you're saying that without God, life has no ultimate meaning.

Al: Exactly! Or as another atheist put it, "If there *is* a God, I'd have to change my behavior."

Jo: Change his behavior? What for?

Al: Because in creating us, God had a very definite purpose in mind —a purpose that he wants us to achieve.

Jo: Could you repeat one last time, in simple terms, just what that purpose is?

Al: Certainly. And I'll do so by quoting what I learned back in grade school—the answer to the question in our catechism book, "Why did God make me?"

Jo: And the answer?

Al: "God made me to know him, to love him, and to serve him in this world, so that I can be happy with him forever in the next." Notice the order Jo, you can't love someone, until you know the person. And to prove your love, you want to do what the person you love wants—that is, through service. And that's how we achieve happiness—both in this life and in the next.

Jo: Yeah, that seems to make sense.

Al: I'd like to wrap up this discussion by quoting Ignace Lepp—a former atheist and Communist. It summarizes perfectly everything I've said. After becoming disillusioned with life, he wrote:

> "What could I do with a life that was no longer animated by an ideal? I followed the recipe of distraction. But the pleasures I discovered gave me no real happiness. More than once I asked myself, 'Rather than continue a meaningless life, would it not be better to end it all?
>
> "Neither the hereafter nor my own immortality concerned me. I now questioned myself about the meaning of life. It did not seem logical that beings endowed with the capacity for thinking and loving could be thrown into an absurd universe, where there was nothing to think, nothing to love, nothing to hope for.
>
> "It was with these dispositions that I came upon the Christian message."[3]

And that will be the goal for our future discussions, to review the Christian message.

Man's Search for Meaning

This section takes its title from a bestseller written by Dr. Viktor Frankl, a Viennese psychiatrist. After World War II, Frankl recounted his experiences as a prisoner in various Nazi concentration camps. His parents, his wife and his brother died in those camps; only he and his sister survived.

One may wonder—having lost everything he valued in life and under constant fear of the gas chamber—how could he find life worth living? Would it not be better to end it all by taking his own life, as so many other prisoners had done?

It was due to his suffering in those camps that he came to his hallmark conclusion that even in the most dehumanized situations, life has potential meaning, and that suffering can be meaningful. The following account of an experience which he had while confined at Auschwitz is an example of Frankl's idea of finding meaning in the midst of extreme suffering:

"... We stumbled on in the darkness, over big stones and through large puddles... The accompanying guards kept shouting at us and driving us with the butts of their rifles... Hardly a word was spoken; the icy wind did not encourage talk. Hiding his mouth behind his up-turned collar, the man marching next to me whispered suddenly: 'If our wives could see us now! I do hope they are better off in their camps and don't know what is happening to us.'

"That brought thoughts of my own wife to mind. And as we stumbled on for miles, slipping on icy spots, supporting each other time and again, dragging one another up and onward, nothing was said, but we both knew: Each of us was thinking of his wife. Occasionally I looked at the sky, where the stars were fading and the pink light of the morning was beginning to spread behind a dark bank of clouds. But my mind clung to my wife's image...I heard her answering me, saw her smile, her frank and encouraging look. Real or not, her look was then more luminous than the sun which was beginning to rise.

"A thought transfixed me: for the first time in my life I saw the truth—that love is the ultimate and the highest goal to which man can aspire. Then I grasped the meaning of the greatest secret that human poetry and human thought and belief have to impart: The salvation of man is through love and in love. I understood how a man who has nothing left in this world may still know bliss, be it only for a brief moment, in the contemplation of his beloved...' "[4]

Later on in his book, Frankl cites the example of Jerry Long as "a living testimony to the defiant power of the human spirit. To quote the *Texarkana Gazette,* 'Jerry Long has been paralyzed from the neck down since a diving accident which rendered him a quadriplegic three years ago. He was 17 when the accident occurred.

"Today Long can use his mouth-stick to type. He 'attends' two courses at Community College via a special telephone. The intercom allows Long to both hear and participate in class discussions... And in a letter I received from him, he writes: 'I view my life as being abundant with meaning and purpose. The attitude that I adopted on that fateful day has become my personal credo for life: I broke my neck, it didn't break me. I am currently enrolled in my first psychology course in college. I believe my handicap will only enhance my ability to help others. I know that without the suffering, the growth I have achieved would have been impossible.' "[5]

Compare the example of Jerry Long's achievements with what Frankl cited a few pages earlier: "I am reminded of the findings presented by Annemarie von Forstmeyer who noted that, as evidenced by tests and statistics, 90 percent of the alcoholics she studied had suffered from an abysmal feeling of *meaninglessness.* Of the drug addicts studied by Stanley Krippner, 100 percent believed that 'things seemed *meaningless.*' "[6] [emphasis added]

*   *   *

In his *Confessions*, St. Augustine captures the theme of Doctor Frankl's book in one short sentence:

"Our hearts were made for you, O Lord,
and they are restless until they rest in you."

3. How Can You Tell What's True?

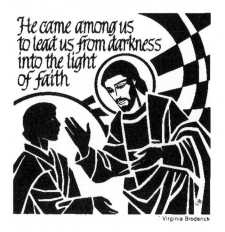

He came among us to lead us from darkness into the light of faith

Virginia Broderick

Jo: What's on the agenda for today?

Al: Truth!

Jo: You mean religious indoctrination.

Al: Not really. We base our lives on what we think is true. The question is, how do we arrive at what's true?

Jo: From personal experience.

Al: That's one way. It's now raining. So if I say the sun's shining, you could tell me I'm wrong. Our present experience contradicts me.

Jo: What's the other way to arrive at truth?

Al: From the experience of others, that is, from witnesses. For example, who was President during the Civil War?

Jo: Lincoln.

Al: How do you know? You weren't there.

Jo: That's what I read in the history books.

Al: Good! We take the word of those who were there and made a record of it. They are witnesses and we can put faith in them.

Jo: There you go again, bringing religion into this.

Al: Relax! Faith is just taking someone else's word for an event we have not experienced. We can't live without at least some faith.

Jo: For example?

Al: You place an order in a restaurant. When the waiter brings your meal, how do you know that the cook hasn't poisoned the food?

Jo: Because I trust the person.

Al: That's what I mean by faith. In this case, you believe that a cook you don't know has prepared your soup without adding arsenic. I repeat: we cannot live our lives without at least some faith.

Jo: OK. I'll grant you that we need some natural faith; but I don't buy any of that religious stuff.[7]

Al: Before continuing, tell me: How do we learn the most important things in life? From our own experience or from that of others?

Jo: From our own personal experience.

Al: I disagree. You don't even know who your parents are, unless you take their word for it.

Jo: Nonsense! My birth certificate tells me that they're my parents.

Al: Years ago, most adopted children were not told that they were adopted. The birth certificate listed the adoptive parents as the biological parents. So for the most important fact about yourself, you have to take someone else's word for it.

Jo: And if that someone else lies to me, that proves my point. The only sure way to know what's true is from personal experience.

Al: Or when you do take someone else's word, be certain that the witness is reliable.

Jo: That can't be done with absolute certainty.

Al: I'm not *absolutely* certain that the roof over us won't collapse in two minutes. But I'm *morally* certain that it won't. To lead a normal life, the best we can hope for is *moral* certitude. Otherwise, we wouldn't get out of bed in the morning.

Jo: And how can you tell a truthful witness from one who's lying?

Al: We investigate items like:
—Was the witness present for what happened?
—Does he have something to gain from lying?
—Can we verify the facts from other sources?
—The more witnesses, the more reason to accept the evidence.

Jo: That only proves what I've held all along. The Bible is just a book of myths.

Al: On the contrary, the historical books of the Bible are *real* history.

24

Jo: There's not one original book of the Bible—I mean, the actual text written by the author.

Al: That's true. But there are no originals of any book from ancient times. Only copies—all of them manuscripts (= handwritten).

Jo: Then how can you be sure that copying mistakes didn't creep into the text over the course of centuries?

Al: Because of the number of copies that we have. Take Caesar's *Gallic Wars*, for example. There are only ten manuscripts, and the earliest one dates from 950 AD. But for the Bible we have over 5,000 manuscripts, and the oldest one is from 350 AD. We even have some verses of John's gospel from the year 130 AD.

Jo: You still don't have any way to prove that the original authors didn't fabricate the events reported.

Al: We sure do. To distinguish fact from fiction, we have internal as well as external evidence.

Jo: External evidence?

Al: Yes. For example, some folks deny Jesus ever existed. They say he's mentioned only in the Bible. That bias ignores the witness of Josephus, a Jewish historian—to say nothing of what the pagan historians Suetonius, Tacitus and Pliny say about Jesus.

Jo: You say that some pagan historians mention Jesus?

Al: That's right. In 115 AD, Tacitus describes the great fire that destroyed Rome in 64 AD. To squelch the rumors that *he* had started the fire, the emperor Nero pinned the blame on "those whom the people call Christians. Pontius Pilate had *Christus*, the leader of this sect, condemned to death in the reign of Tiberius. This superstition broke out in Judea, and then made its way to Rome, where all shameful things wind up…"

Jo: Give me another example.

Al: Suetonius tells how the emperor Claudius expelled all the Jews from Rome around 50 AD. That supports what Acts 18:2 says: "Paul met a Jew named Aquila, who had recently come from Italy because Claudius had ordered all Jews to leave Rome."

Jo: You say there's internal evidence too. What does that refer to?

Al: Reliable historians show both the strengths and the flaws of a person's character. Wouldn't you doubt a historian's objectivity if he reported the strong economy under President Clinton, but omitted his affair with Monica Lewinski or his impeachment trial?

25

Jo: You bet I would!

Al: Well, we read in the Bible that David, the greatest king of Israel, committed adultery with Bathsheba. Then to cover it up, he had her husband, Uriah, murdered. Isn't it safe to conclude that the other incidents reported in 2 Samuel are also factual?

Jo: Yes, I'd say that the author was reliable.

Al: The same applies to the Gospels. The apostles often come across as dimwitted, petty and jealous. And the night that Jesus was arrested, Simon Peter *cursed* and *swore* that he had never laid eyes on the man. Talk about flaws!

Jo: I get your point.

Al: Then take the phrase, "the Son of Man." With two exceptions, it's found in the New Testament only on the lips of Jesus. It's his preferred way of referring to himself—more than forty times.

Jo: So what?

Al: St. Paul wrote most of his letters before the Gospels. And in his letters, he calls Jesus "the Christ, the Lord, the Savior, and Son of God," but not once does he call him "the Son of Man." The fact that only Jesus uses that title is strong internal evidence that the authors were accurate in what they reported.

Jo: So what are you driving at?

Al: That the historical books of the Bible are reliable. We should accept them as valid history, just as we do the other books of history that have come down to us from the ancient world.

> Jesus is the central theme of the whole Bible.
> The Old Testament says, "The Messiah is coming!"
> The New Testament says, "He has arrived!"
> And that's the topic of our next discussion.

A World Without Truth
by Matthew Kelly[8]

There is genius in Catholicism, but the world doesn't see it that way. Today's secular culture rejects the Catholic worldview and instead chooses relativism as its champion. Relativism is the most insidious philosophy of our age. It steals away all meaning from life, and in doing so robs us of the joy God wants us to live with. Joy is simply not possible without meaning. Pope Benedict XVI said this about it: "Relativism, which considers all opinions true even if they are contradictory, is the greatest problem of our time." Think about that for a moment. Consider all the problems of the world today, and yet he says relativism is the greatest of all of them.

So, what is relativism? It is the theory that there are no absolute truths, but rather all truths are relative. That is, something that may be true for you may not necessarily be true for me. This leads to an environment in which every person can do whatever he or she wants to do. This philosophy is full of contradictions, because the idea that nothing is absolute is itself an absolute statement. Relativism is usually confined to the area of morals and ethics. In other areas relativists will concede that everything scientifically verifiable is true, but that anything that cannot be scientifically verified is not. The problem is, you cannot scientifically verify this statement. Relativism holds that it is true for everybody that nothing is true for everybody. That, of course, is a self-contradictory proposition.

The problem is that most of us don't think enough about life, and little bits of errant philosophies like relativism can stick to us easily enough as we make our way through this world. They are presented under the guise of being open-minded or tolerant. But it is good to be close-minded about certain things—even before you try them. I am close-minded about putting my hand in a chainsaw.

Relativists will say you cannot impose your morality on others, that you cannot legislate your personal beliefs. But if you saw someone beating a child, wouldn't you try to stop that person? Some things are right and some things are wrong, but relativists will not concede this. And doesn't all legislation impose someone's personal beliefs (or a group's personal beliefs) on the whole society? There is no moral way to sympathize with immoral actions, and it is necessary to be intolerant of some things. Besides, you don't tolerate things that are good, right? You don't have to. You only have to tolerate things that are unpleasant.

If humanity is to make any progress in [this] century, the error of moral relativism must come to an end. And the only way to remove this insidious philosophy from our world is to root it out of our lives, one person at a time, starting with you and me. Now we come face-to-face again with the central rule that personal transformation plays in the incredible plan God has for our lives and the world. You can only rid the world of relativism by ridding individuals' lives of it one at a time. The transformation of a society and the transformation of the individuals who make up that society are inseparable.

One of the most beautiful lines I have ever read is the opening of John Paul II's *Veritatis Splendor* (The Splendor of Truth): "The splendor of truth shines forth in all the works of the Creator, and in a special way, in man, created in the image and likeness of God. Truth enlightens man's intelligence and shapes his freedom, leading him to know and love the Lord."

What Is Truth?

by Archbishop Charles J. Chaput[9]

Aleksandr Solzhenitsyn was a great moral witness of the twentieth century, who began as an atheist but ended Russian Orthodox.

In 1978, four years after Solzhenitsyn left Russia, he was invited to speak to the graduating class of Harvard University. What Harvard may have expected was praise for Western abundance, freedom, and diversity. What it got was very different.

Solzhenitsyn began by noting that Harvard's motto is *Veritas*. This is the Latin word for "truth." Then he added that "truth is seldom pleasant; it is almost invariably bitter."

Then he spent the next 6,000 words saying what nobody wanted to hear. He methodically criticized Western cowardice and self-indulgence; the vanity and weakness of America's intellectual classes; the "tilt of freedom in the direction of evil;" the right of people "not to have their divine souls stuffed with gossip, nonsense [and] vain talk" by the mass media; a pervasive Western atmosphere of legalism and moral mediocrity; and the rise of a destructive individualism that now forces decent people "to defend not so much human rights as human obligations."

Some of Solzhenitsyn's hard words came from his suffering. Some flowed from loneliness for his own country. But while Solzhenitsyn was harsh in his comments at Harvard, he also was accurate in at least some of what he said. Speaking of his Russian homeland he said, "After suffering decades of violence and oppression, the human soul longs for things higher, warmer and purer" than anything offered by the practical atheism now common in the West.

The reason for the problems of the West, said Solzhenitsyn, is found "at the root, at the very basis of human thinking in the past [several] centuries." Our culture has fallen away from our own biblically informed heritage. We've lost the foundation for our moral vocabulary. This loss has starved our spirit, debased our sense of any higher purpose to life, and destroyed our ability to defend or even to explain any special dignity we assigned to the human person in the past.

28

4. Does the Bible Make Sense?

The law of the Lord is perfect – refreshing the soul

Virginia Broderick

Al: Jo, are you convinced the historical books of the Bible are reliable?

Jo: Sort of. But the Bible doesn't make much sense. It seems to be crammed with contradictions.

Al: Do you understand the theme that runs through the whole Bible?

Jo: Which is?

Al: That God directly intervened in our world to save us from the power of sin and death.

Jo: Sorry, but I don't buy it.

Al: Do you remember our first discussion?

Jo: What about it?

Al: Can you say that you love someone, if you're forced to?

Jo: Of course not!

Al: You're right. God gave us free will so that we could prove our love for him. That's why he tested our first parents by ordering them not to eat from the tree of the knowledge of good and evil. But they abused their freedom and turned their backs on God.

Jo: It sounds like a fairy tale to me.

Al: But it's the truth. As I've said already, you don't need the Bible to prove original sin. All the evil in the world indicates that something is intrinsically wrong in human nature.

Jo: Adam and Eve mess up, so God blasts them. How vindictive!

Al: Breaking physical laws has consequences. If I ignore the law of gravity by walking off a cliff, I'm going to suffer irreparable harm. Likewise, if I disobey the moral law, I'm going to pay the price. It follows from the misbehavior, not from God.

Jo: So you won't admit that God causes evil.

Al: Never! Even when our first parents sinned, God didn't cut them off. He promised a Savior. That's what the Bible is all about.

Jo: You make it sound so simple.

Al: It's not simple, but certainly reasonable. Let's start with Genesis 3:15. That's right after Adam and Eve sinned. God tells Satan, in the guise of a serpent, what's in store for him. Here, read it.

Jo: God said: "I will make you and the woman enemies. Your offspring and hers will also be enemies. He will crush your head, while you snap at his heel." What's that supposed to mean?

Al: God is predicting that there's going to be war between Satan and the woman's offspring ("seed"). Who do you think the woman is?

Jo: Must be Eve. She's standing right there.

Al: Adam is there, too—and a patriarchal culture always favors the male. Besides, this is the only time where Scripture attributes "seed" ("*sperma*") to a woman. No, God is referring to a specific woman whose son will one day crush Satan's power over us.

Jo: And who might that be?

Al: Mary, the mother of Jesus. In his letter to the Galatians, St. Paul says as much: "When the time finally arrived, God sent his Son, born of a woman, born under the Law of Moses." (Gal 4:4)

Jo: So God's Son was Jewish?

Al: When he became man, yes! That's the main point of the whole Old Testament.

Jo: I still don't get it.

Al: Early on, everyone was a polytheist.

Jo: Meaning that they worshipped many gods.

Al: Correct. About 2,000 years before Christ, God called Abraham and said: "I am the only true God. I'm going to make you the father of a great people—my chosen people—the Jews."

Jo: Do you expect me to believe that God really chose the Jews?

Al: Tell me, where are the Hittites today?

Jo: I don't follow you.

Al: The Hittites lived in Palestine at the same time the Israelites did. But where are they now?

Jo: I haven't a clue.

Al: They're not! On the streets of New York you'll meet any number of Jews—but not a single Hittite. Of all the ancient peoples who occupied the Holy Land, only the Jews have survived to this day. So in preserving them, God had a special purpose in mind.

Jo: Which was?

Al: To assert two facts: a) He alone is the one true God, and b) One of their own was going to be the promised savior of the world.

Jo: And is that why God called Abraham?

Al: Yes! He made a covenant with him, promising, "In your seed— that word *sperma* again—every nation on earth will be blessed." A famine 200 years later forced the Hebrews to settle in Egypt.

Jo: And they settled there?

Al: They did until the Egyptians enslaved them. Then God raised up Moses to lead them back to the land he had promised them.

Jo: Is that why the Jews claim Israel as theirs?

Al: Yes. But more importantly, God made a covenant with them on Mt. Sinai, where he again promised to send them a savior. He kept renewing that promise through all the prophets he sent.

Jo: Are you implying the prophets predicted the arrival of Jesus?

Al: Yes, accurately, in great detail. Here are some Old Testament prophecies. You read them, and I'll explain each one.

Jo: **Gen 49:10** "The royal staff will not depart from Judah until the one it belongs to, arrives." (1600 BC)

Al: Jacob had twelve sons, whose offspring made up Israel's twelve tribes. Here God is excluding all the other tribes except Judah's.

Jo: **2 Sam 7:12-13** The Lord said to David, "I will appoint one of your descendents to be the King... I will establish his royal throne forever." (950 BC)

Al: About 1,000 years before Christ, God eliminated all the clans of

Judah except for David's. He told King David, "Your offspring will be the savior, and he will reign forever." Jesus fulfills that promise on both counts. He's from David's bloodline, and he is still ruling.

Jo: Still ruling? Where?

Al: In heaven and in the hearts of his followers. He split all history right down the center—BC and AD. Like it or not, we are all stamped with the year of his birth. Our calendars mark the actual year of his reign—for example, 2015. The next quote, please.

Jo: **Isaiah 7:14** "Behold, the virgin[10] will be with child and bear a son and she will name him Emmanuel." [= God-with-us] (700 BC)

Al: That promised sign came true in Mary, who by saying "Yes" to God's plan, conceived Jesus through the power of the Holy Spirit with no intervention from a human father. Matthew and Luke narrate the details in the first two chapters of their gospels.

Jo: **Micah 5:2** "Bethlehem, out of you will come the one who will rule over Israel for me. His origins go back to days of eternity."

Al: 700 years before his birth, God foretold that the Messiah would be born in Bethlehem—the birthplace of King David.

Jo: **Zechariah 9:9** "Rejoice, Jerusalem! See, your King is coming to you…gentle and riding on a donkey."

Al: 500 years later that promise came true, as Jesus, mounted on a donkey, entered Jerusalem with everyone shouting, "Hosanna!"

Jo: **Psalm 22:15-18**
"All who see me mock me, hurling insults at me…
    My tongue sticks to the roof of my mouth…
They have dug holes in my hands and my feet,
    I can count every one of my bones…
They divide my garments among them,
    and for my cloak they cast lots …."

Al: Composing that psalm over 900 years earlier, King David predicted what Jesus was going to suffer on the cross:
    —the mockery of the bystanders
    —the excruciating thirst
    —the nails through his hands and feet
    —the soldiers gambling for his garments

Jo: **Psalm 16:9-10**
"My body will rest in safety,
    for you will not abandon my soul to the grave,
    nor will you allow your Holy one to see corruption."

Al: Here, we have another one of David's psalms. Pre-Christian Rabbis applied this text to the Messiah. It was fully realized in the bodily resurrection of Jesus. Yes, it's all there, just as the gospels describe it some 900 later.

Jo: It almost seems rigged.

Al: Someone could conceivably "fix" an event or two of his life to fit some prophecies. But the odds for the same man fulfilling these and many other prophecies in his person are astronomical. No! Jesus *is* the Messiah, promised hundreds of years beforehand.

* * *

Albert Einstein:
"As a child, I received instruction both in the Bible and in the Talmud. I am a Jew, but I am enthralled by the luminous figure of the Nazarene... No one can read the Gospels without feeling the actual presence of Jesus. His personality pulsates in every word. No myth is filled with such life... No man can deny the fact that Jesus existed, nor that his sayings are beautiful..."[11]

From the Second Vatican Council:
"Holy Mother Church has firmly and with absolute constancy maintained and continues to maintain, that the four Gospels just named, whose historicity she unhesitatingly affirms, faithfully hand on what Jesus, the Son of God, while he lived among men, really did and taught for their eternal salvation, until the day he was taken up... The sacred authors, in writing the four Gospels, selected certain of the many elements which had been handed on, either orally or already in written form, others they synthesized or explained with an eye to the situation of the churches, the while sustaining the form of preaching, but always in such a fashion that they have told us the honest truth about Jesus."
—*Dogmatic Constitution on Divine Revelation,* No.19

The Bible: A Love Letter from God

This afternoon, I stopped by to visit Charles Held and his wife Harriet—a beautiful couple in their 80s, both confined to wheelchairs. While discussing the Bible, Charles began to reminisce. He recalled an incident that had taken place 50 years earlier at the Presbyterian Youth Camp.

One of the campers that summer was a teenager by the name of Dennis. At the youth meetings that he attended during the previous school year, Dennis had become infatuated with a teenager named Dolores. The only problem was that in June, Dolores' family had to move to California—a move that separated her from Dennis by some 3,000 miles.

At youth camp one afternoon right after mail call, Charles is driving a busload of campers to an outing. In the rearview mirror he notices that Dennis is intently reading a letter he has just received at mail call—and he continues to read it throughout the entire forty minute ride. At their destination, Dennis was the last one to exit the bus.

Charles called out after him, "Dennis, either that's the longest letter ever written, or you're the world's slowest reader. Now, which is it, son?"

"Aw, Mr. Held, you wouldn't understand. This letter is from someone very special—someone I love. And I just can't read it enough times."

Then from his wheelchair, Charles concluded, "You know, Father Victor, he was right. I could have read that same letter and it would not have meant a thing to me. Why not? Because the author of the letter meant nothing to me—I didn't know her.

"It's the same with Holy Scripture—God's love letter to us. Many people complain that when they try to read the Bible, it sounds like so much gibberish. Well, it's no wonder! They still don't know the author of that beautiful love letter. Because if they did, they just couldn't read enough times."

From my Journal – 14 Feb 1996 + Victor Galeone

Yes, Holy Scripture is God's love letter to us. Make the decision now to immerse yourself into that marvelous message. Begin with John's Gospel. Read a short passage every day for at least ten minutes—inserting a card to mark the place where you'll continue the following day.

The more you learn about Jesus, the more you will love him. And the more you love him, the more happiness you'll experience in life.

"Ignorance of the Scriptures is Ignorance of Christ."
St. Jerome (c. 341-420)

5. Jesus: Lunatic, Liar, or Lord?

Christ
became
obedient
for us
even to
death

© Virginia Broderick

Jo: What's on your mind for today?

Al: I'd like us to examine some of the claims that Jesus made.

Jo: Claims about what?

Al: About himself—and who he was.

Jo: That's easy. He was the carpenter from Nazareth—who became a wandering preacher.

Al: That's right. But he also made some astounding claims that a normal, devout Jew would never have made.

Jo: Like what?

Al: Like claiming to be on a par with God—the same God that the Jews worshipped.

Jo: He did no such thing.

Al: He sure did. Recall the time they brought that paralyzed man to him. Jesus looked at him and said, "Son, your sins are forgiven."

Jo: So? I can forgive others for the wrong they've done to me.

Al: For the wrong they've done to you, yes. But not for what they've done to someone else. That's the whole point. As his listeners objected, "What arrogance! Only God can forgive sins."

Jo: That's true. How did Jesus explain that one?

Al: In substance he said: "Talk comes easy. But to prove to you that I do have the power to forgive sins on earth," he said to the paralyzed man, "Get up and go home." And the man did.

Jo: One robin doesn't mean that it's spring.

Al: We're not talking about a single instance. There are countless times that Jesus said what no sane Jew would ever say.

Jo: For instance?

Al: Tell me, where does the commandment about honoring one's parents occur in the list of the Ten Commandments?

Jo: I think right after the ones that deal with God.

Al: That's right. Yet Jesus has the boldness to say, "Whoever loves father and mother more than me is not worthy of me." He's placing himself above the most important relationship that we have on this earth. He's placing himself in the realm of God!

Jo: You're reading too much into that.

Al: Not so. Take the commandment that deals with keeping the Sabbath day holy—the day that belongs to God alone. What does Jesus affirm? He makes the bold statement, "I am Lord even of the Sabbath." (Mt 12:8)

Jo: But didn't Jesus say that he did not come to destroy the Law of Moses—just to fulfill it?

Al: He did. But again, notice how he fulfills it. Imagine that we have an old-fashioned scale.

Jo: The type with a pan on each side?

Al: Yes. On one side, Jesus quotes God's commandment, "You shall not kill." On the other side, he puts, "But I say to you: Don't even get angry with your brother...." There's no balance at all. The word "but" gives more weight to his words than to God's! And he does the same with, "You shall not commit adultery."

Jo: Hmm, maybe so. He seems to be upstaging God.

Al: Now you get my point. Here's another one from Isaiah 40:8,
"The grass withers, the flower fades,
    but the word of our God endures forever."
— Now read what Jesus says in Mark 13:31.

Jo: "Heaven and earth will pass away,
    but my words will never pass away."

Al: His words are eternal—just like God's! Besides, several times Jesus claimed to have existed before his life here on earth.

Jo: That's impossible.

Al: I'm merely trying to show that Jesus repeatedly implied he was equal to God.—Let's go to John's gospel, chapter 8. Jesus is in a heated debate with the Jewish leaders. In verse 56, he tells them: "Your father Abraham rejoiced at the thought of seeing my day. He saw it and was glad."—Mind you, Abraham lived some 2,000 years earlier! Now read how they reacted.

Jo: They said to him: "You're not even 50 years old. How could you have seen Abraham?"

Al: Now read the answer Jesus gave.

Jo: "I'm telling you the truth: Before Abraham was even born, I AM." —That's bizarre. What strange talk!

Al: It is, until you realize that "I AM" is the divine name God revealed to Moses in the burning bush. Recall what God told Moses: "My name is I AM. Tell the Israelites: I AM has sent me to you."—So Jesus is claiming to be one with the Great I AM—God himself!

Jo: Did his listeners take it that way too?

Al: Why else did they pick up stones to throw at him? In the same vein, if a man is on trial for his life, would he tell a deliberate lie on the witness stand, a lie that could incriminate him?

Jo: Only if he's insane.

Al: Would you say that Jesus was insane?

Jo: No, I don't think anyone would say that.

Al: Well let's go to Jesus' trial before the Jewish high court in Mark 14:55. His judges want him executed. But their witnesses fail to supply a capital offense. So Jesus takes the stand and is put under solemn oath. Now read what the high priest asked.

Jo: "Are you the Messiah, the Son of the Blessed God?"

Al: To which Jesus responds: "I am! Moreover, you will see me, the Son of Man, sitting at the right hand of Almighty God and coming on the clouds of heaven." How did the judges react?

Jo: It says that the high priest tore his robe apart, shouting, "Why do we need more witnesses? You just heard the blasphemy! What is your verdict?" And they all agreed that he should die.

Al: Do you know why the high priest tore his robe? It was a ritual action, whenever a Jew heard someone claim a prerogative that belonged to God alone. Check it out in 2 Kings 5:7.

Jo: But I don't see anything in Jesus' answer that implies he was claiming a right that was exclusively God's.

Al: Actually, he claimed it twice. First, the right side is the place of honor. It's reserved only for one's superior or for one's equal. So what is Jesus implying by saying he will be sitting at God's right?

Jo: I guess he's implying, "I'm God's equal."

Al: Absolutely! And the second divine right that Jesus claims is that he will return at the end of time on the clouds of heaven.

Jo: What's so special about clouds?

Al: In our culture, nothing. But to the Jewish mind, clouds indicate the presence of God, they're his chariot, and his alone (see Psalms 104:3). Also, recall the cloud covering Mt. Sinai and the meeting tent whenever God came down to speak with Moses.

Jo: So you're insisting that Jesus claimed to be equal to God?

Al: That's right. At his trial before Pilate, the Jewish leaders admitted as much: "We have a law that says he must die for claiming to be the Son of God." (Jn 19:7)

Jo: OK. But just claiming equality with God doesn't mean it's true.

Al: You have three choices: He was deluded, or demonic, or divine.

Jo: Or just a great moral teacher!

Al: But a great moral teacher would never claim to be God unless, of course, he really was.

Jo: Why not?

Al: C.S. Lewis expressed it best in his book, *Mere Christianity*:[12]

"A man who was merely a man and said the sort of things Jesus said wouldn't be a great moral teacher. He would either be a lunatic or else he would be the devil of hell.

"You must make your choice. Either this man was and is the Son of God, or else a madman or something worse. You can shut him up for a fool, you can spit at him and kill him as a demon; or you can fall at his feet and call him Lord and God. But let us not come with any patronizing nonsense about his being a great human teacher. He hasn't left that open to us. He didn't intend to."

The Shroud of Turin

The Holy Shroud is a 14-foot linen cloth with the frontal and dorsal image of a nude man who appears to have been physically traumatized by crucifixion. It is kept in the royal chapel of the Cathedral in Turin, Italy. Composed of faint shades of brown, the image is barely visible to the naked eye.

The existence of the Shroud can be historically traced to France, where it was in the possession of Geoffroi de Charney in the year 1357. The Knights Templar came to possess it in the sack of Constantinople during the Fourth Crusade. Prior to that, it was identified with the Image of Edessa, dating back to the fourth century. John's gospel chapter 20 vv. 6-7, refers to the burial cloths of Jesus which Peter and John discovered on entering the tomb on Easter morning.

In 1898, Secondo Pia, an amateur photographer, was allowed to photograph the Shroud for the first time as part of a rare exhibit in the Turin Cathedral. Later, developing the negative in his darkroom, he almost dropped the photographic glass plate—so shocked was he to see the image of a face on it. His negative was in fact a "positive" image of the brown shadows on the Shroud.

Actual Image of face on Shroud - Negative image of Shroud face

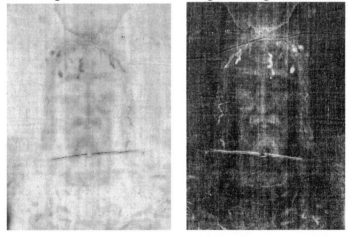

In other words, the entire image on the Shroud is a negative, with the exception of the bloodstains, which are positive. Furthermore, it is not a painting. Various experts testing the Shroud detected no pigments. The image is the result of a scorch on the surface of the linen, similar to a burn mark left on a shirt from an overheated iron.

The Shroud and Carbon-14 dating

In 1988 the Vatican granted permission for specimens of the Shroud to be tested via carbon-14 analysis by three universities to ascertain its age. The results dated the Shroud between the years 1220 and 1390. However, more recent research shows that the material used in the 1988 analysis was cut from a medieval patch woven into one end of the Shroud to repair damage caused by a 1532 fire. "The radiocarbon sample has completely different chemical properties than the main part of the Shroud relic," said Raymond Rogers, a retired chemist from the Los Alamos National Laboratory. To date, the Vatican has not permitted a new analysis.

Could the Shroud be a hoax?

If so, then we must answer:

- How did a forger create a negative picture centuries before the discovery of photography? And why would a forger have left the bloodstains positive?
- Why did he locate the nail hole in the wrist instead of the palm of the hand, as almost all artists do to this day? (A nail driven in the palm cannot support the full weight of a suspended adult body.)
- There are no thumbs visible on the hands of the figure on the Shroud. How would a forger know that a spike, driven through the wrist, forces the thumb to bend flush into the palm of the hand—a reflex action caused by the median nerve?
- Why would a medieval forger depict the victim completely naked? The buttocks are visible on the dorsal side, while on the frontal side the hands are folded over the groin.
- How did a forger get pollen specimens from plants that grow only in the vicinity of Jerusalem and in Turkey? Max Frei, a Swiss criminologist, discovered pollen on the Shroud from plants native to those two areas, as well as to France and northern Italy.
- And how could a forger so accurately replicate the scourge marks all over the victim's body from a Roman *flagellum*—a weapon common at the time of Christ?

Jewish Shroud Expert: "It's authentic!"[13]

In 1978, the Shroud of Turin Research Project (STURP) team conducted the first in-depth scientific examination of the Shroud of Turin. Barrie Schwortz was the official documenting photographer for STURP. In an interview conducted by Zenit.org in March 2012, he said, "At the very beginning of my involvement with the Shroud, I was very skeptical about its authenticity. I had no emotional attachment to Jesus or to the subject matter since I was raised an Orthodox Jew."

Schwortz became convinced that the Shroud was authentic when another team member, Allen Adler, who was also Jewish and a blood chemist, explained to him why the blood remained red on the Shroud instead of turning black or brown. Schwortz added, "Adler was involved in this, not so much from a religious point of view as from a scientific point of view...It came as a shock to me after almost 20 years that this piece of cloth was authentic."

Schwortz concluded: "For me, once I came to the conclusion from science that it was authentic, I came to understand...[that] this is like a forensic document of the Passion; and for Christians around the world this has got to be the most significant relic because it accurately documents everything that is told in the Gospels of what was done to Jesus."

You may visit Schwortz's website at www.shroud.org.

* * *

The Triumph of the Cross
by St. John Chrysostom[14]

[Jesus] was bound, betrayed by an apostle, spat upon, outraged with insults, scourged, nailed to the cross, and—as far as some were concerned—he did not deserve to be buried in a tomb. His executioners divided his garments. They suspected that he aspired to be a king and he died for it. "For everyone who makes himself king, sets himself against Caesar." They suspected him of blasphemy, and he died for it. "Behold, you have heard his blasphemy!"

Even though he would undergo all these torments, he roused up those who would listen; he stirred them to courage by saying, "Do not be afraid because of what they did to me. I was crucified, I was scourged, I was outraged and insulted by robbers, I was arrested on suspicion of blasphemy and of being a king. But after my death and resurrection, people will look on my sufferings in such a way that no one will say that they were not filled with abundant value and honor."

Certainly, this did come to pass. And [Isaiah] predicted it long beforehand when he said: "On that day, the root of Jesse will stand as an emblem for the nations. The nations will put their trust in him, and his resting place shall be glorious." This kind of death is more glorious than a crown. Certainly, kings have laid aside their crowns and taken up the cross, the symbol of his death. On their purple robes is the cross. On their crowns is the cross. At their public prayers is the cross. On their weapons is the cross. On the sacred table of their altar

41

is the cross. Everywhere in the world, the cross shines forth more brightly than the sun. [For as the prophet said above:] "And his resting place shall be glorious."

In human affairs, things do not generally happen that way. Persons of distinction flourish while they are alive; but after they die, their exploits are reduced to nothing. Anyone can see how true this is, not only in the case of the wealthy and of rulers, but even in the case of the emperor himself. Their laws are abrogated; their images obscured; people's memory of them is blotted out; their names are forgotten; those who once enjoyed their favor are now held in scorn. This is the lot even of those emperors who waged wars, of those who, by a single nod changed the condition of peoples, cities, and affairs; of those who had the power to put men and women to death, of those who could give a reprieve to all on their way to execution. But all their great powers have perished, despite the great honors shown to them while they were alive.

With Christ it is quite the opposite. Before the Cross, his situation was one of shame and dejection. Judas betrayed him. Peter denied him; the others fled. He stood alone and was led off in the midst of his many foes. Many who had believed in him now deserted him. But after he died on the cross, his situation was not destroyed but became brighter, more glorious and more sublime. From this you should understand that the crucified one was no mere man.

6. The Resurrection: Fact or Fiction?

He is risen as He promised

Virginia Broderick

Al: Jo, are you now convinced that Jesus claimed to be on a par with the one true God?

Jo: All right. I'll admit that he claimed to be God. But that doesn't prove that he was.

Al: Yes, even a fool can claim to be God—Jesus proved his claim.

Jo: And how did he do that?

Al: By his resurrection—the fact that he came back to life the third day after he was crucified.

Jo: His followers invented that story.

Al: Tell me, Jo, who discovered America?

Jo: Columbus.

Al: You weren't there; so how do you know?

Jo: From those who were. The sailors who accompanied Columbus saw what happened. They recorded it in the ship's log. And from there it made its way into our history books.

Al: Precisely! Reliable witnesses convinced you that Columbus discovered America. And that's why I believe that Jesus rose from the dead: because of reliable witnesses!

Jo: How do you know that his followers didn't fabricate that story?

43

Al: For three reasons:
1. They didn't embellish what they reported.
2. They included some very embarrassing details.
3. They died for what they were proclaiming.

Jo: You're going to have to prove that.

Al: Okay. First, let's verify that Jesus really died.

Jo: A good place to start. Some skeptics say he just faked his death.

Al: Before crucifying him, they beat him to a pulp with whips, making him so weak that someone had to help him carry the cross.

Jo: Yet when he was supposedly dying, he was strong enough to cry out in a loud voice!

Al: True. But the soldiers who marveled at that, were the very ones who certified his death.

Jo: How so?

Al: Since they wanted to shorten the agony, they broke the legs of the two criminals on either side of Jesus. But when they saw that he was already dead, they didn't break his legs. Instead, a soldier ran a spear into his side, and out came blood and water. He was dead, all right. So dead—that they buried him in a tomb.

Jo: Maybe his followers stole the body.

Al: Get serious! When Jesus was arrested and still alive—they bolted like a bunch of cowards. Now that he's dead and gone, you want me to believe that they came under cover of night to steal the corpse? For what purpose?

Jo: To support their hoax.

Al: Okay. Let's pretend that they stole the body and made up the story about the resurrection. Don't you think they would have invented a more credible account of what happened?

Jo: What do you mean?

Al: In all four gospels, who were the first ones to discover the empty tomb on Easter morning?

Jo: The women. They wanted to finish embalming the body—or so the legend has it.

Al: And where were the apostles?

Jo: By their own account, in the upper room.

Al: Imagine, the apostles behind locked doors in the upper room for fear of the Jewish authorities! Does that make sense?

Jo: Why not? It's all a lie anyway.

Al: If they were lying, why did they add such embarrassing details? The "brave" apostles are scared stiff, while the women—the so-called "weaker sex"—are at the scene of the action!

Jo: Yeah, that is sort of strange.

Al: Besides, back then, women could not act as witnesses in a court of law. If the apostles fabricated a hoax, they did a poor job of it.

Jo: People in those days were a lot more gullible.

Al: On the contrary, when the women discovered that the tomb was empty, they concluded that someone had stolen the body.

Jo: Where does it say that?

Al: John's gospel says that Mary Magdalene ran to the upper room to tell Peter and John, "They have taken the Lord from the tomb and we don't know where they have put him."

Jo: So they thought he was still dead?

Al: They sure did.

Jo: What made them change their minds?

Al: For forty days, Jesus appeared to them on and off in different places and under various circumstances.

Jo: They were hallucinating.

Al: For one of them to hallucinate—perhaps! But for all eleven apostles to be hallucinating at the same time—impossible!

Jo: Just denying it doesn't make it so.

Al: Actually, the first time Jesus appeared to them, the apostles thought they *were* hallucinating. They cried out, "It's a ghost!"

Jo: See that!

Al: Hey, when you're really deluded, you think you're experiencing a real ghost. Jesus had to prove he was alive by having them touch his hands and feet—telling them: "Touch me and see. A ghost doesn't have flesh and bones, as you yourselves can feel."

Jo: I don't buy it. It all sounds too neat.

Al: Neat! Thomas wasn't there the first time Jesus came. So when the others told him they had seen Jesus, he didn't believe them.

Jo: When one of his own apostles refused to believe he was alive, why do you expect me to?

Al: Thomas insisted on conditions: "Unless I put my finger into the nail holes of his hands, and put my hand into the spear wound in his side, I will not believe." Do you know what happened next?

Jo: I imagine Jesus appeared to them again.

Al: He did, the following Sunday. And he submitted to the terms that Thomas had set up in advance. He had him put his finger into the nail holes, and his hand into the spear wound.

Jo: And did that convince him?

Al: It sure did! He fell to his knees and cried out, "My Lord and my God!" Do you know what Jesus said next?

Jo: I have no idea.

Al: "Because you've seen me, Thomas, you believe." What was it that Thomas believed?

Jo: That Jesus was back to life again.

Al: Jo, I don't *believe* that you're sitting in front of me—I *know* it. We believe what we can't see. And we cannot see divinity. The gospel text says very clearly Thomas believed that Jesus was God: "Thomas said to *him*, 'My Lord and my *God!*'"

Jo: So you're insisting that because Jesus rose from the dead, that proves that he was God.

Al: Coupled with the fact that he *claimed* to be God—yes! You see, God would never have brought an imposter back to life.

Jo: I still can't shake the conspiracy theory. The only ones who claimed that they saw him alive again were his followers.

Al: You're forgetting about Saul—later named Paul. He never laid eyes on Jesus before his death on the cross. Yet one minute he's killing Christians; and the next, he becomes one of them.

Jo: What brought about the change?

Al: Jesus appeared to him. A fictitious analogy would be if Hitler, in the midst of the Holocaust, had become a Jew and had himself circumcised, claiming that the God of Abraham, Isaac, and Jacob had appeared to him.

46

Jo: Maybe Paul saw only the spirit of Jesus.

Al: Not so! As an ex-Pharisee, Paul believed in the resurrection of the body on the last day.[15]

Jo: I still don't see how Jesus had the same physical body as before, since he could go right through locked doors.

Al: It *was* the same body—but in a glorified form. Consider this: Water, H2O, can appear in three different forms: liquid, solid or vapor. But it's still water—H2O—in all three forms. It's the same with Jesus' body. Before he died, it was mortal, subject to the laws of nature. After rising, it was immortal and glorified—two different forms, but one and the same body.

Jo: And you say that that's what made Paul become a Christian—because he actually saw Jesus in his glorified body?

Al: Exactly! And like all the other apostles, he died for his beliefs.

Jo: A Muslim will die for what Mohammed taught. Does that make Islam true?

Al: You'll die for what you believe, only if you're convinced it's true. You'll never give up your life for what you know is a hoax.
    The difference between a Muslim today and the apostles back then, is that they were in a position to know the truth. For unlike today's Muslims who never saw Mohammed in the flesh, the apostles ate and spoke with Jesus after he had risen from the dead. If they were not absolutely certain that he had risen, they would never have let themselves be tortured to death for insisting that they had seen the risen Lord.

He Is Risen

This book began with the inspirational reflection, "One Solitary Life." After summarizing the life of Jesus from his birth to his burial, it immediately refers to the central place that Jesus occupies in world history.

But one basic fact is missing. Minus that fact, Jesus would have been a mere nonentity. Do you know what's missing? His resurrection! It's the linchpin of his entire life.

The enemies of Christianity attempt to dismiss the resurrection as a hoax concocted by Jesus' disciples. They allege that the disciples moved his corpse to another location to support their fabricated lie. Or perhaps they were hallucinating.

St. John Chrysostom, an early Christian writer, refuted all these bogus arguments by countering with the following reasons:

"How do you account for the fact that these men, who deserted and denied Christ during his lifetime, set out to win the whole world for him after his death? Did they perhaps say to themselves, 'He could not save himself while he was alive, but now that he is dead, he will extend a helping hand to us? In his lifetime he brought no nation under his banner, but by uttering his name we will win over the whole world for him.

"It is evident, then, that if they had not seen him risen from the dead and had proof of his power, they would never have risked so much—including their own lives."[16]

St. Paul asserts the same thing in 1 Corinthians 15:14, 19: "If Christ has not risen from the dead, then our preaching is useless, and so too is your faith... If our hope in Christ is for this life only, we are to be pitied more than everyone else."

St. Paul's assertion is valid: "If Christ has not risen from the dead, then our preaching is useless, and so too is your faith..." Faith is a difficult concept to grasp. Perhaps the following reflection might shed some light on it.

On one occasion Jesus told his disciples, "Unless you change and become like little children, you will never enter the kingdom of heaven." (Mt 18:3) What did Jesus mean by that? That children and those who are childlike can grasp the mysteries of the faith better than brilliant scholars? How can that be? Could it be that children still have the capacity to believe in fairy tales? If you think for a moment, the central mystery of our faith sounds very much like a fairy tale:

The prince left his castle in never-never land.
He disguised himself like the poorest in the realm.
He went about doing good to all,
    preaching a message of peace and love:
"If you want to get to my Father's palace,
    there's a narrow, winding road that you must follow."
His opponents turned on him: "Who do you think you are?"
They nailed him to a cross between two criminals.
When he was dead, he was buried in a borrowed tomb.
And as often happens in fairy tales—
    when the prince comes to kiss his beloved back to life—
    so, too, in ours: "On the third day he rose again in glory."

Yes, it does sound like a fairy tale—but with this one difference: It's the fairy tale come true! Jesus is alive! Ultimately, it's due to his bodily resurrection that he is "the central figure of the human race (BC/AD) and the leader of the column of progress."

But Jesus doesn't want to reign just on the pages of a calendar. No! He wants to reign in our hearts. And that brings us to the most important item of this entire book: surrendering your heart to Jesus.

This is exactly what **Pope Francis** asks all of us to do—especially committed Christians—in his Apostolic Exhortation, *The Joy of the Gospel*:

1. The joy of the gospel fills the hearts and lives of all who encounter Jesus. Those who accept his offer of salvation are set free from sin, sorrow, inner emptiness and loneliness. With Christ joy is constantly born anew. ...

2. The great danger in today's world, pervaded as it is by consumerism, is the desolation and anguish born of a complacent yet covetous heart, the feverish pursuit of frivolous pleasures, and a blunted conscience. ...

3. I invite all Christians, everywhere, at this very moment, to a renewed personal encounter with Jesus Christ, or at least an openness to letting him encounter them; I ask all of you to do this unfailingly each day. No one should think that this invitation is not meant for him or her, since no one is excluded from the joy brought by the Lord. The Lord does not disappoint those who take this risk; whenever we take a step towards Jesus, we come to realize that he is already there, waiting for us with open arms. Now is the time to say to Jesus: "Lord, I have let myself be deceived; in a thousand ways I have shunned your love, yet here I am once more to renew my covenant with you. I need you. Save me once again, Lord, take me once more into your redeeming embrace." How good it feels to come back to him whenever we are lost! Let me say this once more: God never tires of forgiving us; we are the ones who tire of seeking his mercy. ...[17]

In the last book of the Bible, St. John quotes Jesus in glory saying: "Behold, here I stand at the door and knock. If anyone hears my voice and opens the door, I will come in to eat with him and he with me." (Rev 3:20)

In the late 1800s, an Austrian artist painted that scene of Jesus knocking on the door. When the painting was first put on display, a friend commented to the artist, "You forgot to paint the latch on the door." The artist replied: "This door has only one latch—on the inside —because it's the door to the heart."

49

Jesus respects our freedom. He will not force his way into our hearts. We must invite him in willingly. If you don't know how, tell him so in your own words—and be honest. Say something like this:

> "Lord Jesus, I need you. I'm so sorry for all those times that I turned my back on you. Just thinking about all the crud that I've been messing around with fills me with shame. Please forgive me, because from now on I want to love you. Yes, I surrender my heart to you. I never again want to become bitter, or angry, or selfish, or give into those lustful desires. Please help me, Lord, because without your support, I'll just keep on sinning—and falling into deeper and deeper depression."

On waking up every day, get into the habit of praying this aspiration:

"Jesus, I love you!
Come into my heart and stay with me all day long."

Extra Incredible

A popular argument used by atheists is called the "extraordinary claim argument." It says that an extraordinary claim (like the Resurrection of Christ) requires extraordinary evidence. It is a clever way of setting the bar so high that, no matter what kind of evidence the Christian presents, the atheist does not even have to deal with it.

The next time somebody tries this gambit on you, remember that it cuts both ways. The idea that this wonderful, intricately designed, and finely tuned universe randomly popped into existence out of nothing for no reason and then proceeded to organize itself through random, purposeless processes—is that not an extraordinary claim? The notion that Christ's disciples were transformed from clueless wimps and cowards into people who turned the world upside down by what they knew to be a lie—is that not an extraordinary claim?

And the idea that atheists are the only ones who care about reason and evidence, while Christians are the ones who believe absurdities out of blind faith—that may be the most extraordinary claim of all!

—Donald T. Williams

From *Touchstone Magazine,* Sept-Oct 2014, p. 6
Reprinted with the author's permission
(website: http://doulomen.tripod.com)

7. The Trinity: an Assault on Reason?

ⓒ Virginia Broderick

Jo: Al, I had some visitors come to my door the other day.

Al: What did they want?

Jo: They asked me if I believed that Jesus was God. I told them that I thought so.

Al: And their reaction?

Jo: They said: "If Jesus was really God, then the Creator of the entire universe was in a woman's womb for nine months. It means the Almighty crawled on his hands and knees as an infant. Do you truly believe that's the case?" I didn't know how to answer them.

Al: You didn't? Well, you should have. Yes, God was in a woman's womb for nine months! And yes, God did crawl on his hands and knees as an infant. That's what we mean by the Incarnation.

Jo: The Incarnation? Is that in the Bible?

Al: The word isn't, but the concept is. It's from a Latin word that means "into-flesh". It refers to God's one and only Son becoming one of us, when he took on our mortal flesh in Mary's womb.

Jo: You mean that the Son of God took the place of Jesus' soul?

Al: No! Jesus had a human soul just as he had a human body. He was a real human being just like us.

Jo: Well wouldn't that make Jesus two persons, one human and the other divine?

Al: Jesus is only *one* person, and that person is *divine*. Furthermore, that divine person has two distinct natures.

Jo: I'm confused. Tell me what you mean by a person.

Al: A person is someone who can know and love, that is, endowed with an intellect and a free will.

Jo: That's fine for a philosopher. But it means nothing to the average person on the street.

Al: I disagree. A five-year-old runs up from the basement shouting, "Mommy, somebody's downstairs!" Does he mean an animal?

Jo: Why, no. "Somebody" refers to a person.

Al: You're right!—someone who can know and love. It answers the question, "Who?" Jesus is only one person—a person who was with the Father from all eternity.

Jo: So when he took on our nature in Mary's womb, he became a human person. Right?

Al: Wrong! Let me say it again. There is only *one* person in Jesus and that person is divine. He always existed. But that divine person has two distinct natures—one human and the other divine.

Jo: Explain what you mean by nature.

Al: Nature is the source of our actions. For example, birds can fly but we can't. It's not in our nature.

Jo: And how does nature differ from a person?

Al: Nature says *what* we are; person says *who* we are. Nature is the source of our actions; it's the person who does them.

Jo: When you say that Jesus has two natures, does that mean they combine in him, like hydrogen and oxygen do to form water?

Al: No. They don't combine. Unlike hydrogen and oxygen that lose their individual properties in water, each nature in Jesus— human and divine—maintains its own distinct properties.

Jo: For what purpose?

Al: So that Jesus could be true God and true man—two separate natures in one single person.

Jo: I still don't see the reason for that.

Al: Tell me, can God suffer?

52

Jo: No, I don't think so.

Al: That's right. God, as God, can't suffer. So God's Son became man in order to suffer in his human nature, and thus save us.

Jo: You mean to say that God really suffered?

Al: He did. Since there's only *one* person in Jesus, and that person is divine, then God suffered. It's the person who feels pain. We say, "My tooth is killing me"—*me*, the person!

Jo: Then God's Son really felt pain on the cross?

Al: That's right. If *we* had been beaten with whips and crucified, we would have felt all that excruciating pain. He was beaten with whips and crucified. He—the person—felt it all.

Jo: Did the Father suffer too?

Al: No! Only God the Son became man. You're confusing the persons of the Trinity.

Jo: Trinity? What on earth is that?

Al: It's a convenient term to refer to the relationships that exist in God's inner life.

Jo: Is that in the Bible?

Al: Again, the word isn't, but the concept is. No one has ever seen God. Jesus came to tell us all about him—to reveal God's inner life, as far as it's possible for us to grasp.

Jo: And how did he do that?

Al: Check out these facts:
- Jesus claimed to be equal to the one, true God (see p. 35 ff).
- He called God his Father over 100 times.
- He also called himself God's one and only Son.
- Since there's only *one* God, the Father and the Son must be one and the same God.

Jo: That's impossible! Two separate persons but only one God?

Al: Jesus said as much in John 10:30:
"I and the Father are one." (= one in being)[18]

Jo: That doesn't make any sense.

Al: Jo, are you capable of transferring the entire ocean into a hole that you've dug in the sand at the seashore?

Jo: Of course not!

Al: Then why presume that our limited human mind—like that small hole in the sand—can comprehend the infinite, eternal God?

Jo: But you want me to accept a contradiction—that two equals one.

Al: That three distinct persons are the one selfsame being is not a contradiction. Incomprehensible, yes! Contradictory, no!

Jo: But what does it mean?

Al: Let's take it one step at a time. From all eternity, God knows himself. In that self-knowledge, he conceives the person that St. John calls the "Word" in the very first verse of his gospel."

Jo: What's that supposed to mean?

Al: When a man fathers a son, what's the common link between them that makes them related?

Jo: The sperm. That's the part of the father that connects him biologically with his son.

Al: That's right. But God is Spirit. So when he fathered his Son, he did not give just a part of himself—he gave his entire being to his Son. So now there are two distinct persons who are one and the same divine being. The Son is the Word—the Concept that God has of himself from all eternity. And like the Father, he always existed! The Son is the perfect image of his eternal Father.

Jo: How does the Holy Spirit fit into that?

Al: The Father always loves the Son, and the Son always loves the Father. Their mutual, eternal love is the Holy Spirit.

Jo: You mean to say that he's God too?

Al: Absolutely! Jesus said, "Go…baptize in the name of the Father and of the Son and of the Holy Spirit." If the Father and the Son are God, the Holy Spirit must also be one and the same God.

Jo: I don't see why.

Al: For the same reason that I wouldn't say to you, "Meet my three friends: Peter, Paul and John's *foot*." A normal person would never join three disparate entities in the same breath.

Jo: Is another way to talk about the relationship of the three Persons in the Trinity: Creator, Redeemer, and Sanctifier?

Al: No. And the reason is that those titles depend on the temporal relationship of us human creatures with God—and not on the inner life of the three Divine Persons with one another, which are eternal relationships, and never had a beginning.

54

Note: St. Paul also joins the three persons together many times, as for example, in 2 Corinthians 13:14:
"The grace of our *Lord* Jesus Christ [= the Son],
the love of God [= the Father]
and the fellowship of the Holy Spirit be with all of you."

The Son is listed before the Father, indicating that all three persons are equal.

Also, take note that the New Testament normally uses "God" as the proper name of the Father, and "Lord" as the proper name of the Son.

Is the Trinity Relevant?
by Dr. Marcellino D'Ambrosio[19]

Many are ready to give a polite nod of some sort to Jesus of Nazareth. Most honor him as a great moral teacher. Many even confess him as Savior. But the Incarnation of the Eternal God? Second person of the Holy Trinity? God can't be one and three at the same time. Such a notion is at worst illogical, at best meaningless. "This was all invented by the Roman Emperor Constantine in 313 AD," so scoffs a motley crew ranging from the Jehovah's Witnesses to the Da Vinci Code.

Of course this charge has no historical leg to stand on. St. Ignatius of Antioch wrote seven brief letters around 110 AD in which he called Jesus "God" 16 times.

True, the word "Trinity" is not in the Bible. But everywhere the New Testament refers to three distinct persons who seem to be equally Divine, yet One (e.g., 2 Corinthians 13:13). So over 100 years before Constantine, a Christian writer named Tertullian coined the term "Trinity" as a handy way to refer to this reality of three distinct, equal persons in one God. It stuck.

But if the doctrine of the Trinity is authentically biblical, is it relevant? Does it really matter?

If Christianity were simply a religion of keeping the law, the inner life of the lawgiver would not matter. But if Christianity is about a personal relationship with God, then who God really is matters totally. Common sense tells us that some supreme being made the universe and that we owe Him homage. But that this creator is a Trinity of Persons who invites us to intimate friendship with Himself, we never could have guessed. We only know it because God has revealed it.

God is love, says 1 John 4:8 (see also John 3:16). If God were solitary, how could he have been love before he created the world? Who would there have been to love? Jesus reveals a God who is eternally a community of three persons pouring themselves out in love for one another. The Father does not create the Son and then, with the Son, create the Spirit. No, the Father eternally generates the Son. And with and through the Son, this Father eternally "breathes" the Spirit as a sort of personalized sigh of love. "As it was in the beginning, is now and ever shall be." That's what the conclusion of the Glory Be really means, that the self-giving of the three divine persons did not begin at a moment in time, but was, is, and is to come.

If we are truly to "know" our God, we must know this. But if we are ever to understand ourselves, we must also know this. For we were made in the image and likeness of God, and God is a community of self-donating love. That means that we can never be happy isolated from others, protecting ourselves from others, holding ourselves back selfishly from others. Unless we give ourselves in love, we can never be fully human. And unless we participate in the life of God's people, we can never be truly Christian either. Because Christianity is about building up the community of divine love which is called the Church. If God is Trinity, then there really is no place for free-lance, lone-ranger Christians.

The family, the domestic Church, is a reflection of Trinitarian love—the love of husband and wife, distinct and very different persons, generates the child who is from them but is nonetheless distinct from them, indeed absolutely unique.

And that is the final point. One of the greatest treasures of Western culture is the concept of the uniqueness and dignity of the individual person. You really don't find this idea in the ancient societies of Greece and Rome or in other great world religions, such as Islam.

The concept of the irreplaceable uniqueness of each person came into Western culture straight from the doctrine of the Trinity, three who possess the exact same divine nature but who are yet irreplaceably unique in their personhood.

The irony? As it progressively abandons the triune God, the Western world is undermining the very foundation of personal dignity, individuality, and freedom.

So yes, the Trinity does matter!

8. With the Bible, Who Needs a Church?

guard the rich deposit of faith with the help of the Holy Spirit

©Virginia Broderick

Al: Jo, I haven't seen you for months. What have you been up to?

Jo: I accepted Jesus as my personal Lord and Savior, and then I joined Solid-Rock Church.

Al: Really? What's that church like?

Jo: It's a Bible-believing church.

Al: Meaning?

Jo: Once you've surrendered your heart to Jesus, the Bible alone is your final authority for what to believe. If it's not in the Bible, you don't have to believe it.

Al: Where does it say that in the Bible?

Jo: 2 Timothy 3:16: "All Scripture is inspired by God and is useful for teaching, rebuking, correcting and training in goodness."

Al: That says all Scripture is useful for teaching, rebuking, etc. But that doesn't mean Scripture is the only authority for our beliefs.

Jo: Are you trying to shake my faith?

Al: No. I'm delighted that you found Jesus. I just want you to see that besides the Bible, our faith has to rest on something more.

Jo: Like what?

Al: The authority of the Church.

Jo: So you want me to join your church, do you?

Al: Not my church—It's Jesus' Church!

Jo: The Church came after the Bible. So the Bible is our only authority. Or as Luther said, "Sola Scriptura!" (Scripture Alone!)

Al: Let's concentrate on the New Testament. Go to 1 Corinthians chapter 1, verse 2. Read it, please.

Jo: "To the Church of God which is in Corinth, to those sanctified in Christ Jesus..."

Al: Let's pause right there. When Paul wrote that letter, where was the New Testament portion of the Bible?

Jo: It was in the process of being written.

Al: That's right! And where was the Church?

Jo: It says that part of it was in Corinth.

Al: Right again! In 57 AD, Paul writes a letter to the Corinthians that *will* become part of the Bible. Yet he says: "To the Church which *is* in Corinth." Jo, you've put the cart before the horse. The Church came before the New Testament—not vice versa.

Jo: I disagree!

Al: Please read 1 Corinthians 15:1 for me.

Jo: "Brothers, I want to remind you of the gospel I preached to you,"

Al: That was seven years earlier.

Jo: "...which you believed, and which will save you, provided that you keep believing exactly what I preached to you."

Al: Notice, St. Paul is telling them to keep on believing the gospel he had already preached to them. For the first Christians, saving faith came from preaching—not from the Bible.

Jo: I know that. But once they believed, they needed the Bible to support their faith.

Al: True! But who decided which books to include in the Bible?

Jo: The early Christians just knew.

Al: Not so! Some of them considered the Gospel of Thomas inspired. Others said the book of Revelation wasn't. So again, who made the final decision on which books to include?

Jo: I don't know.

Al: The Church—at the Councils of Hippo and Carthage in the fourth century!

Jo: And who gave them the right to do that?

Al: Jesus himself! In Matthew 18:17-18, Jesus made the apostles the last court of appeals on earth. In the verse that follows, he says quite clearly that whatever decision the apostles made on earth would be ratified in heaven.

Jo: The *apostles*, yes! Not some bishops four hundred years later.

Al: The bishops are the successors of the apostles, and they inherited their authority.

Jo: I don't buy that.

Al: Check out these facts:
- Jesus chose 12 apostles to lead his Church. (Mk 3:13-19)
- He told them, "Go, make disciples of all nations…teaching them to observe all that I have commanded you." (Mt 28:19)
- He then said he would be with them till the end of time. (v. 20) Now how could Jesus be with the apostles until the end of time, if they were going to die?

Jo: I haven't a clue.

Al: Through their successors. Peter chose Matthias to replace Judas. (Acts 1:21) Paul told Titus to appoint "elders in every town to encourage and rebuke with all authority." (Tit 1:5; 2:15) The Book of Acts is nothing else but an account of how the apostles prepared others for the ministry of spreading the faith.

Jo: And what kept them from teaching error?

Al: The Holy Spirit. Here, read these verses from John's gospel. Jesus is speaking to his apostles the night before he died.

Jo: "The Holy Spirit, whom the Father will send in my name, will teach you all things, and remind you of everything I said to you." (Jn 14:26) "I have much more to tell you, more than you can take in right now. But when the Spirit of truth comes, he will guide you into all truth." (Jn 16:12)

Al: See, Jo! Jesus promised to guide the leaders of his Church after he was gone through the Holy Spirit. So it's not the Bible alone.

Jo: But the Bible validated their teaching!

Al: You've got it backwards. They were the ones who validated the Bible. As St. Augustine said: "I would not believe in the Gospel, unless the authority of the Catholic Church moved me to do so."

Jo: There you go again—giving Catholics all the credit!

Al: No more than Luther did. Even after his break with the Church, he admitted: "We are obliged to yield many things to the Papists [Catholics]—for example, that they possess the Word of God, which we received from them. Otherwise, we should have known nothing at all about it."[20]

Jo: I don't care what Luther said! For me, all I need is God's word!

Al: Jo, where do we find the pillar and foundation of truth?

Jo: In the Bible, where else?

Al: That's not what the Bible says. Please read 1 Timothy 3:16.

Jo: "I wanted you to know how people ought to behave in God's family—that is, in the Church of the living God, which is the pillar and foundation of truth."

Al: There you have it, Jo. The Church is the pillar and foundation of truth—not the Bible. Besides, without the Church, how can you tell what a particular Scripture passage means?

Jo: Just from your own private interpretation.

Al: Again, that's not what the Bible says. In Acts 8:30, when the Ethiopian eunuch was reading from the prophet Isaiah, Philip the deacon asked him, "Do you understand what you are reading?" Now read what the eunuch answered him.

Jo: "How can I—unless someone explains it?"

Al: See that! Private interpretation isn't scriptural. St. Peter says the same thing in his second letter: "Remember there is no prophecy in Scripture, which is a matter of personal interpretation. Why? Because prophecy never came from man's effort. When men spoke for God, they were inspired by the Holy Spirit." (2 Pt 1:21-22)

Jo: Do you mean to say that we need the Church to tell us what every verse in the Bible means?

Al: No! Most of it is self-evident. But for a disputed passage, especially in important matters of faith and morals, the Church has to be the final judge.

Jo: I don't see why.

Al: We have the U.S. Constitution that spells out our rights. When there's a dispute about a certain law, you can take your case to court. If you lose, you can appeal—all the way to the Supreme Court, if necessary, until you get a final, definitive opinion.

That's how Jesus set up his Church. The Church is the last court of appeals in deciding serious matters of faith and morals.

Otherwise, with private interpretation of Scripture, you'll have as many churches as you have opinions about what the Bible says—just as we have today!

The Deposit of Faith: Spiritual Riches
by Deacon Don Awalt[21]

An expression that confuses many people is the "Deposit of Faith." Just what does it mean? Perhaps the analogy of a three-legged stool might help. The Deposit of Faith is God's collective revelation that was completed in Jesus Christ. It is represented:

1) in written form through the Bible;

2) in the oral Tradition, passed down to us from the Apostles; and

3) preserved for us by the apostolic succession of our bishops.

All three components are essential to assure the truth of what we believe. Just as a three-legged stool would topple if one leg was missing, so too would the assurance of our faith, if one of the three components of the Deposit of Faith were absent.

St. Paul can serve as an icon for the written tradition of the Bible, since he contributed more to the New Testament through his letters than any other single author. St. Peter stands as an icon for the oral Tradition of the Church, since he carried on the ministry of oral teaching long before the New Testament had been committed to writing. Check out the first half of the Book of Acts, where there are multiple instances of Peter proclaiming the Good News.

The icon for the third leg of the stool is the teaching authority of the bishops—or the Magisterium, as it is officially called. This teaching authority was first given to the Apostles by Jesus, as recorded in Matt 18:18, "I tell you the truth, whatever you forbid on earth will be forbidden in heaven, and whatever you permit on earth will be permitted in heaven." And down through the ages it was the Holy Spirit who guarded the bishops, as the successor of the Apostles, from teaching error: "The Holy Spirit, whom the Father will send in my name, will teach you all things, and remind you of everything that I said to you." (Jn 14:26)

61

There are many who find it very difficult to accept oral Tradition as a true component of the Deposit of Faith. Recall the children's game of passing a secret from one child to another. After being passed along by ten or more children, the final version bears little resemblance to the initial secret. How then are we to accept important points of the Faith that were passed down by word of mouth over long periods of time? In response, the following points should be stressed:

1. St. Paul himself refers to oral Tradition: "So then, brothers, stand firm and hold to the traditions that I taught you, either by word of mouth or by letter."['by letter' refers to 1 Thessalonians] (2 Th 2:15)
2. Also, recall that the inhabitants of the Near East had phenomenal memories as compensation for their lack of reading skills.
3. And passing on the oral Tradition lasted only for a generation or two at most, before it was committed to writing by the early Church Fathers.

A matter that causes serious doubts for others is the lack of integrity by some apostolic leaders and the bishops who followed them over the centuries. Does serious sin invalidate their teaching authority? Both Peter and Paul sinned grievously: Peter by denying Christ and Paul by fiercely persecuting the first believers. Also, in the Second Book of Kings, many of the monarchs were unfaithful, wicked leaders. Were those kings truly God's representatives? And do Church leaders today who are sinful really possess the authority of Christ?

The answer may lie in something said by St. Augustine, who recognized this same concern. Augustine said that God permits tension in our lives in order to test our faith. We are reminded that the Church contains two dimensions: one, natural—redeemed sinners; and the other, supernatural—Christ, our divine Head.

So why does the Church of Christ exist?

First, besides preserving the Deposit of Faith, which has been revealed to humanity by God, the Church exists to ensure that God's Word is both preached and heard. The Church's structure, sacraments, and clergy exist as the place, the means, and the help for us to become more united with Christ.

Next, the Church exists to point one and all towards the Kingdom of God—to make the Kingdom visible, as our ultimate goal in life. As such, the Church exists like a bridge from this world to the life where we shall enjoy the beatific vision of God. We are reminded of this by one of the Pope's several titles, "Pontiff"—Pontifex in Latin, meaning "bridge builder."

Lastly, the Church exists so that God's love for his people may always be evident—the Church is a source of grace from God to the whole human family. Recall the story in Ezekiel 47, where water flows as a trickle from the altar, eventually becoming as deep as a river that can be crossed only by swimming. This water flowing from the altar signifies the grace that flows from the sacraments—gifts of our eternal Father's love! And all of these gifts from God come to us through the Church, the beautiful Bride of Christ.

There is a legend often told in the early Church at Rome, that while many Christians were being rounded up by the forces of the Emperor Nero for martyrdom, St. Peter was stealthily fleeing the city on the Via Appia. Along the way, he encounters Christ walking in the opposite direction towards the city. Peter asks him, "Lord, where are you going?" Jesus replies, "To Rome, to be crucified again." With both shame and a heightened resolve, Peter returned to Rome, where he was soon captured and met his end by being crucified in Nero's Circus on the Vatican Hill.

Today is a good day to ask ourselves, "Where are we going?" If our answer is not "With Christ!", then today is a great day to turn back to God. Christ and his Church are there to help us!

What's in a Name?
By Sheldon Vanauken [22]

Catholic, Protestant, and Orthodox alike claim the name of *Christian*, first used at Antioch (see Acts 11) for the disciples—the *believers*—who accepted the teaching of the Apostles. It did not mean nice people, moral when convenient; it meant believers. But believers in what? That Jesus was a good man, preaching a beautiful but impossible system of morality? Or perhaps a prophet, like Isaiah? No: they were believers that Jesus was the Christ (hence *Christian*), the Son of God, God made flesh.

How can we define in the fewest possible words what a *Christian* is and, if different, what a *Catholic* is? It is, of course, true that to define is to limit; ... A dog is a dog and not a cat. ... And a *Christian* is a believer that the Christ is God Himself become a Man—who was killed and then in body rose from the dead. Firm and clear. If you believe that, you are a Christian. If not, not. Those who think of Jesus as merely a dead teacher of morality are not Christians and ought to have a different [title]... The Catholics, Orthodox and Evangelicals who share this enormous faith far greater than their real differences— should stand together as fellow Christians against the secular world.

63

But what is it that sets *Catholic Christians* apart? Once again in the fewest possible words—a minimal definition—what specifically is a Catholic? First of all, he is a Christian as defined. It has been pointed out that Protestants retain a very Catholic understanding of the Incarnation and the Trinity, but what they have lost is all understanding of the meaning of the Church. The Church is, in a word, what makes Catholics different. A Catholic Christian, therefore, must be defined as a believing Christian who further believes that the Universal Church was founded by Christ on the rock that was Peter, to be guided infallibly by the Holy Spirit on matters of faith and morals, to stand like a rock indeed against the energy of human skepticism. That belief is the mark of the Catholic Christian. Those who call themselves Catholics but do not believe that the Church under Our Lord the Spirit is the arbiter of faith and morals have simply ceased to be Catholics.

It is often pointed out that there have been sinful, immoral popes, as though that denied the guidance of the Holy Spirit. What is remarkable is not what the good popes did, but what the bad popes did not do: They did not attempt to alter or twist the faith and morals in all the nearly 2000 years of the Church. The more one thinks about its history, the harder it is to doubt that the Holy Spirit does guide the Church in faith and morals.

But Catholic belief in the Church does not prevent all believing Christians from standing together against the anti-Christ.

9. Who Needs a Pope if You Have Jesus?

Peter the apostle-
Paul the preacher-
teach us
to know
the law of
the Lord

©Virginia Broderick

Jo: Why do you Catholics make such a fuss over the pope?

Al: Because he's the head of the Church—just as the President is the head of our country.

Jo: Well, for me, Jesus is the head of the Church, not the pope.

Al: Yes, Jesus *is* the head of the Church. But before returning to heaven, he appointed a visible head to speak in his name here on earth until he returns in glory.

Jo: Where does it say that in the Bible?

Al: Turn to John 1:42. That's where Jesus meets Simon Peter for the first time. And the very first thing he did was to change his name from Simon to Rock. ["Kepha" = "Petros" = Peter = Rock]

Jo: So?

Al: For the Jews, a name was equivalent to a nickname. It indicated your role in life. Buffalo Bill got his moniker not for killing turkeys, but buffalos. Recall that Jesus' name means "savior" since he was to save us from our sins. (Mt 1:21)

Jo: What's that got to do with the pope?

Al: The Old Covenant names God "Rock" over 40 times. Why, then, did Jesus rename Simon the Rock? For the answer we have to go to Matthew 16:18. Here, read what it says.

Jo: Jesus said to him: "You are Peter [meaning rock] and on this rock I will build my Church. Death itself will never destroy it."

Al: What does that verse mean to you, Jo?

Jo: It means that Jesus will build his Church on *faith*, just like the faith that Peter expressed in the previous verse, when he said, "You are the Messiah, the Son of the Living God!"

Al: Well if there was no new role for Simon to fulfill, why did Jesus bother changing his name to Rock? Besides, Jesus' symbol for faith is a tiny mustard seed, not a mighty rock. No! Peter is the rock on which Jesus intended to build his Church.

Jo: Not so! I heard that it says in Greek: "You are *Petros* and on this *petra* I will build my church." They're two different words!

Al: Jesus spoke Aramaic, which has *Kepha* both times—just as in French: "You are *Pierre* and on this *pierre* I'll build my Church."

Jo: Then why isn't *petra* used both times?

Al: For the same reason that a boy's name is Mario—not Maria. In Greek, *petra* is feminine. *Petros* is just its masculine form.

Jo: St. Paul calls Jesus the rock. (1 Cor 10:4) And in the same letter, he says that Christ is the only foundation. (1 Cor 3:11)

Al: Right! Jesus is the Rock and the Church's main foundation. But he's no longer visible here on earth. That's why, after he rose from the dead, he appointed Peter as his visible representative, his prime minister on earth, if you will.

Jo: Show me where the Bible says that!

Al: In John chapter 21 Jesus appears to seven disciples, including his favorite John. Three times he asks only Peter, "Do you love me?" On answering "Yes", Jesus tells him, "Feed my lambs. Feed my sheep."—Jo, who do the sheep belong to?

Jo: To Jesus, of course. He refers to them as "*my* sheep."

Al: Then why doesn't he feed them himself?

Jo: I suppose because he was getting ready to return to heaven.

Al: Precisely! And that's why he put Peter in charge—to shepherd his flock while he was no longer visibly present on earth.

Jo: All the apostles were to shepherd Jesus' flock! Peter is no better than they are.

Al: He isn't? Then why is he named first all four times that the Twelve are listed—just as Judas' name is always last?

Jo: Mere coincidence. Besides, Paul doesn't agree that Peter was the leader. He rebuked him for being in the wrong in Gal 2:11.

Al: Did the prophet Nathan think he was superior to King David because he had to rebuke him for his sin? Besides, in the previous chapter, Paul admitted Peter's superiority. He made a special trip to Jerusalem "to *consult* with Peter for 15 days," while he barely mentions the apostle James in passing.

Jo: Well, maybe at times Peter did act as the leader. But that ended with his death. I still don't see how the Pope fits into all of this.

Al: You're forgetting what Jesus said about a building. A *building* is only as strong as its *foundation.* Check out the story of the two builders in Matthew 7. When the hurricane struck—the house built on sand collapsed, but the other one did not. Jesus himself gives the reason why not. Here—read what he says.

Jo: "...because it was built on rock." (Mt 7:25)

Al: That's right, Jo. So if Jesus promised that his Church is to last till the end of time ("Death itself will never destroy it"), its rock foundation has to last just as long. The rest is history. Peter brought the Gospel to Rome and was martyred there. He was the first bishop of Rome. For 2,000 years, the bishop of Rome—the pope—has been Peter's successor.

Jo: There's no evidence that Peter was ever in Rome.

Al: Then how do you explain the words at the end of his first letter? "The Church in Babylon sends you greetings." The early Christians used *Babylon* as a code name for *Rome*, as, for example, in Revelation chapter 17 verses 5 and 9.

Jo: Peter never brought the gospel to Rome!

Al: Scripture doesn't say who did. We know it wasn't Paul. In fact, that's the very reason he gives for not visiting Rome sooner: "It has been my aim never to preach the gospel where Christ was known. I did not want to build on someone else's foundation." (Rom 15:20, 22) History identifies that "someone else" as Peter.

Jo: I refuse to buy that.

Al: The early Christian writers are unanimous:
Origen in 240 AD: "Peter was crucified at Rome."

Irenaeus in 180 AD: "But since it would take too much space to enumerate the bishops in all the churches; it's enough to do so for the Church of Rome, the greatest and most venerable of all, founded by the apostles Peter and Paul. For every Church throughout the world is bound to bring itself into line with the Church of Rome, because of her greater guarantees. For in that Church, what the apostles taught has always been preserved by those who govern."[23]

Jo: Forgeries! But you won't dupe me. For me it's Jesus and his saving word in the Bible!

Al: Tell me: Before Luther, where was the Church of Jesus?

Jo: It sure wasn't in Rome!

Al: Then where was it?

Jo: After the early persecutions, paganism corrupted the Church. It took Luther and Calvin to restore her to her original beauty.

Al: Then Jesus never kept his promise to be with his Church "all days, even to the end of the world." (Mt 28:20) Do you expect me to agree that for 1,200 years the Church was nonexistent?

Jo: Surely, you don't expect me to believe that the likes of an Alexander VI with his illegitimate children, or a Julius II with his plundering army were the leaders of Jesus' Church!

Al: If the very first pope denied Jesus with curses and cut off the servant's ear with a sword, does it surprise you that at times some other popes have followed his bad example?

But since you'll accept only what's in the Bible, please examine Jesus' family tree in Matthew chapter one: **Judah** committed incest. **David** was guilty of adultery and murder. **Solomon**, the wisest of kings, gave himself to womanizing and idolatry. **Manasseh** flooded Jerusalem with much innocent blood.

Mind you, these were the leaders of God's chosen people. Yet for the very reasons that you reject the papacy, you should also conclude: "Surely, these sinful men could never have been the ancestors of the incarnate Son of God!"—Yet they were!

May I say one final thing, Jo? St. Ambrose said it in 395: "Jesus said to Peter: 'You are the Rock and on this rock I will build my Church.' And so where you have Peter, you have the Church. And where you have the Church, you have eternal life."[24]

68

Two Witnesses Named Thomas

Thomas More (1535)[25]

One of the most eloquent testimonies of the primacy of Peter ever given was that of Thomas More at his trial on July 1, 1535. The court had found him guilty of high treason for refusing to take the oath of supremacy, which acknowledged Henry VIII as the Supreme Head of the Church of England. In his own defense, More stood before the court and declared: "Seeing that ye are determined to condemn me, (only God knows how) I will now...speak my mind plainly and freely touching my Indictment and your Statute.

"...as this Indictment is grounded upon an Act of Parliament which is directly repugnant to the laws of God and his Holy Church, the supreme government of which...no temporal Prince may presume by any law to take upon himself, since it rightfully belongs to the See of Rome, a spiritual preeminence that was granted by special prerogative by the mouth of our Savior himself, personally present upon earth, only to St. Peter and his successors, bishops of the same See. [This Indictment] therefore, is insufficient in law to charge any Christian man."

And for proof thereof...More declared that this realm, being but one member and small part of the Church, might not make a particular law disagreeable with the general law of Christ's universal Catholic Church, any more than the City of London, being but one poor member of the whole realm, might make a law against an Act of Parliament to bind the whole realm... "No more might this realm of England refuse obedience to the See of Rome than might a child refuse obedience to his own natural father."

Lord Chancellor Audley, who presided at More's trial, commented that it was strange that More should hold his opinion contrary to the considered opinions of the all Bishops and Universities of the realm. To which More responded:

"If the number of Bishops and Universities be so material as your Lordship seems to take it, I am not bound to conform my conscience to the Council of one realm against the general Council of Christendom. For I have, for every Bishop of yours, over one hundred. And for one Council or Parliament of yours, I have all the Councils made these thousand years. And for this one kingdom, I have all other Christian realms."

When More finished speaking, the Lord Chancellor pronounced the sentence of death.

More was beheaded a few days later on July 6, declaring on the scaffold, that he died, "the King's good servant, but God's first."

Thomas Macaulay (1840)[26]

There is not, and there never was on this earth, a work of human policy so well deserving of examination as the Roman Catholic Church. The history of that Church joins together the two great ages of human civilization. No other institution is left standing which carries the mind back to the times when the smoke of sacrifice rose from the Pantheon, and when camelopards and tigers bounded in the Flavian amphitheatre [the Coliseum].

The proudest royal houses are but of yesterday, when compared with the line of the Supreme Pontiffs. That line we trace back in an unbroken series, from the Pope who crowned Napoleon in the nineteenth century to the Pope who crowned Pepin in the eighth; and far beyond the time of Pepin the august dynasty extends.

The republic of Venice came next in antiquity. But the republic of Venice was modern when compared with the Papacy; and the republic of Venice is gone, and the Papacy remains. The Papacy remains, not in decay, not a mere antique, but full of life and youthful vigor.

The Catholic Church is still sending forth to the farthest ends of the world, missionaries as zealous as those who landed in Kent with Augustine, and still confronting hostile kings with the same spirit with which she confronted Attila. The number of her children is greater than in any former age. Her acquisitions in the New World have more than compensated her for what she has lost in the Old.

Her spiritual ascendency extends over the vast countries which lie between the plains of the Missouri and Cape Horn, countries which, a century hence, may not improbably contain a population as large as that which now inhabits Europe. The members of her communion are certainly not fewer than a hundred and fifty millions; and it will be difficult to show that all the other Christian sects united amount to a hundred and twenty millions.

Nor do we see any sign which indicates that the term of her long dominion is approaching. She saw the commencement of all the governments and of all the ecclesiastical establishments that now exist in the world; and we feel no assurance that she is not destined to see the end of them all.

She was great and respected before the Saxon had set foot on Britain, before the Frank had passed the Rhine, when Grecian eloquence still flourished in Antioch, when idols were still worshipped in the temple of Mecca. And she may still exist in undiminished vigor when some traveler from New Zealand shall, in the midst of a vast solitude, take his stand on a broken arch of London Bridge to sketch the ruins of St Paul's.

10. Mary: Ever Virgin and Mother of God?

To do your will, God is my delight – and your law is within my heart

©Virginia Broderick

Jo: Why do you Catholics say that Mary was always a virgin?

Al: It's not just Catholics. Luther and Calvin also believed that Mary was a virgin throughout her life.

Jo: They did? Where did they get that?

Al: From Scripture, check Luke 1:26-38. That's where the Angel Gabriel tells Mary that she's going to have a child—the Savior. Do you know what her reaction was? Here, read it.

Jo: She asked, "How can that happen, since I don't know man?"

Al: In the Bible, to "know man" is a euphemism for having sexual relations. We already know from verse 27 that Mary was promised in marriage to Joseph. Do you think they were planning to consummate their marriage after the wedding?

Jo: Why wouldn't they?

Al: From Mary's objection, "since I don't know man." Look at it this way. Let's say that I offer you a beer but you respond, "Sorry, I don't drink." When do you plan to start drinking?

Jo: Never.

Al: Or I offer you a cigarette but you answer, "No thanks, I don't smoke." Does that mean "just for today?"

Jo: No—it means that I never plan to smoke.

Al: Well, doesn't Mary's answer, "I don't know man," fall into the same category? Did she ever plan to have marital relations? The early Christian writers concluded that Mary and Joseph must have made a private vow to live as brother and sister after their wedding. When Gabriel explained that she was to conceive through the power of the Holy Spirit, Mary gave her consent at once. She remained a virgin for the rest of her life.

Jo: What about Jesus' brothers and sisters, named in Mark 6:3?

Al: In Hebrew, the word brother ('ak) can mean more than just a blood brother. It can also mean half-brother, stepbrother, uncle, nephew, cousin, neighbor, or co-religionist.

Jo: Give me an example from the Bible.

Al: Genesis 12:5 identifies Lot is the son of Abraham's brother—namely, his nephew. But in the next chapter, Abraham says to Lot, "Let us not quarrel, for we are brothers." (Gen 13:8)

Jo: So you're saying that those brothers and sisters of Jesus were just close relatives?

Al: Exactly! Besides, if Mary had other children, why would Jesus, dying on the cross, have entrusted her to his favorite disciple John? "Then Jesus said to the disciple, 'There is your mother.' After that, the disciple took her into his own care." (Jn 19:27)

Jo: Just a moment! Matthew 1:25 says that Joseph did not have relations with Mary until she gave birth to her son. Doesn't that word "until" imply that they had marital relations afterwards?

Al: Once again, we're dealing with the Hebrew way of expressing things. In English, what is said before until is usually not true afterwards: "I didn't drive until I was 21."

Jo: "Until" always works that way in English.

Al: Not always. For example, "Behave yourselves until I get back." Does that mean that the kids can tear the house apart once their mother returns home?

Jo: So in Hebrew, what comes before "until" continues afterwards?

Al: It depends. Hebrew emphasizes only what happens before the "until" clause. What is stated may or may not be true afterwards. Take Psalm 110. God tells the Messiah to sit at his right hand, "until I subdue all your enemies." Does that mean the Messiah must vacate his place of honor afterwards?

Jo: No! Jesus must reign there forever!

Al: Well, Matthew 1:25 is the Hebrew way of stressing that Joseph had nothing to do with Jesus' conception. In other words: "He had no relations with her at any time before she bore a son."

Jo: Give me one more example.

Al: 2 Samuel 6:23 says: "Michal had no children until the day she died." Does that mean Michal give birth while in the grave?

Jo: What about Luke 2:7? It says Mary "gave birth to her firstborn Son." If he's the first, there must have been others after him.

Al: "Firstborn (bekor)" is a technical Hebrew word that conferred special legal status on the firstborn son. As St. Jerome said: "Firstborn doesn't mean that there were any later-born. It merely excludes any previous-born."

Jo: Just saying that doesn't make it so!

Al: Archeology supports St. Jerome. In 1922 a Jewish bride's tomb from 5 BC was unearthed in Egypt, which bore the inscription: "Fate has ended my life in the birth pangs of my firstborn son."[27]

Jo: You mean the first Christians thought Mary was always a virgin?

Al: That's right. As St. Jerome said: "We believe that God was born of a virgin, because we read it in Scripture. We do not believe that Mary had relations after she brought forth her son, because we do not read it in Scripture. Nor do we say this in order to condemn marriage; for virginity itself is the fruit of marriage..."

Jo: You Catholics also call Mary the Mother of God. Doesn't that make her a goddess?

Al: No, she's still a creature—though the greatest of all creatures.

Jo: But to be God's mother, she would have to exist before him.

Al: Tell me, is Mary the mother of Jesus?

Jo: Of course she is!

Al: And do you believe that Jesus is truly God?

Jo: I certainly do!

Al: Then you should admit that Mary is the mother of God—of God the Son only—not of God the Father or of God the Holy Spirit.

Jo: Not so! She's only the mother of Jesus.

Al: Then according to you, Jesus would have to be two persons—one human, and the other divine.

Jo: No! Jesus is only one person—the second person of the Trinity.

Al: Well, when a woman becomes a mother, she's the mother of a person, not of a human nature, isn't she?

Jo: I don't follow.

Al: Let's say that a woman introduces herself to you by saying, "Hello. I'm the mother of Jane's body." How would you react?

Jo: I'd say that she had freaked out!

Al: Right! A woman becomes the mother of a person ("I'm *Jane's* mother."), even though she only gives her child its body. Mary gave Jesus what every mother gives her child: conception, birth and nourishment. Since Jesus is only one person and that person is divine, then Mary is the Mother of God.

Jo: Then why doesn't the Bible say so?

Al: It does. Right after Mary conceived Jesus, she went to visit her relative Elizabeth. The first thing Elizabeth asked was, "And how have I deserved this visit from *the mother of my Lord*? (Lk 1:43)

Jo: One last question. Why do you Catholics honor Mary so much?

Al: Because God honored her first by having her bring his Son into the world. Besides, aren't you failing to do what Mary—under divine inspiration—prophesied would happen: *"From now on, all future ages will call me blessed."* (Lk 1:48)

Let me close with this quote from **Bishop Fulton Sheen**:

"God who made the sun, also made the moon. The moon does not take away from the brilliance of the sun. All its light is a reflection from the sun. The moon would be only a burnt out cinder if it were not for the sun.

"The blessed Mother reflects her divine Son. Without him she is nothing...

"On dark nights, we are grateful for the moon. When we see it shining, we know there must be a sun. So too in this dark night of the world, when men turn their backs on him, who is the Light of the World, we look to Mary to guide our feet while we await the sunrise."

*   *   *

74

Mary - The Second Eve
A reflection by Blessed John Henry Newman[28]

After quoting a number of the early Church Fathers, who refer to Mary as the "Second Eve"—just as St. Paul referred to Jesus as the "Second Adam" in Romans 5:12-20—Cardinal Newman goes on to apply the analogy as follows:

By the **Immaculate Conception** of the Blessed Virgin is meant the great revealed truth that she was conceived in the womb of her mother...without original sin...To her, grace came from the first moment of her being, as it had been given to Eve.

It is so difficult for me to enter into the feelings of a person who *understands* the doctrine of the Immaculate Conception, and yet objects to it, that I am [hesitant about speaking] on the subject....

Does not the objector consider that *Eve* was created, or born, *without* original sin? Why does not *this* shock him? Would he have been inclined to *worship* Eve in that first state of hers? Why, then, Mary?

We do not say that [Mary] did not owe her salvation to the death of her Son. Just the contrary, we say that she, of all mere children of Adam is, in the truest sense, the fruit and the purchase of His Passion. He has done for her more than for anyone else. To others He gives grace and regeneration at a *point* in their earthly existence; to her from the very beginning.

We do not make her *nature* different from others.... She and we are both simply saved by the grace of Christ.

If Eve was raised above human nature by that indwelling moral gift which we call grace, is it rash to say that Mary had a greater grace? And this consideration gives significance to the Angel's salutation of her as "*full of grace*", an interpretation of the original word which is undoubtedly the right one, ...

And if Eve had this supernatural inward gift given her from the first moment of her personal existence, is it possible to deny that Mary too had this gift from the very first moment of her personal existence? ...and it really does seem to me bound up in the doctrine of the [early] Fathers, that Mary is the **Second Eve.**

Cardinal Newman addresses the matter of Mary's **Assumption** *into heaven or her* **Exaltation**, *as he calls it:*

I shall take what perhaps you may think a very bold step,—I shall find the doctrine of Our Lady's present Exaltation in Scripture. I mean to find it in the vision of the Woman and Child in the twelfth chapter of the Apocalypse [the Book of Revelation]....

"A great sign appeared in heaven: A woman clothed with the Sun and the Moon under her feet; and on her head a crown of twelve stars. And being with child, she cried travailing in birth, and was in pain to be delivered. And there was seen another sign in heaven; behold a great red dragon ... And the dragon stood before the woman who was ready to be delivered, that when she should be delivered, he might devour her son. And she brought forth a man child, who shall rule all the nations with an iron rod; and her son was taken up to God and to His throne. And the woman fled into the wilderness." ....

No one doubts that the **"man-child"** spoken of is an illusion to Our Lord; why then is not **"the Woman"** an allusion to His Mother? ...

Not only Mother and Child, but a serpent has not been found in Scripture since the beginning of Scripture, and now it is found at its end. Moreover, in this passage in the Apocalypse, as if to supply... what was wanting in its beginning, we are told for the first time, that the serpent in Paradise was the evil spirit [Satan].

But if all this be so, if it is really the Blessed Virgin whom Scripture represents as clothed with the sun, crowned with the stars of heaven, and with the moon as her footstool, what height of glory may we not attribute to her? And what are we to say of those who through ignorance, run counter to the voice of Scripture, to the testimony of the Fathers, to the traditions of East and West, and speak and act contemptuously towards her whom the Lord delights to honor?

11. The Church: the Body of Christ

Be
intent
on
things
above

your
life is
hidden
now with
Christ
in god

©Virginia Broderick

Jo: A while back we learned that the church is just as necessary as the Bible. But, there's something I still don't understand.

Al: And what's that, Jo?

Jo: I see where it says in the Creed, "I believe in the holy Catholic Church." What's that supposed to mean?

Al: Good question! In the original Greek, the word "church" means an *assembly* or *congregation*. And "catholic" is the Greek word for *worldwide*. So the Catholic Church refers to the Christians of all the local churches worldwide, who believe in Jesus, the Son of God, as their Savior, and who follow his teachings.

Jo: Does that mean you have to belong to the Church of Rome?

Al: We'll examine that when we discuss baptism. First, let's consider how Jesus and the writers of the New Testament used different images to describe the concept of this universal assembly or church. A major one is "The kingdom of heaven (or of God.)" Here, read this story. It's one of Jesus' parables.

Jo: "The kingdom of heaven is like a net cast into the sea that caught all kinds of fish. When it was full, the fishermen hauled it ashore. Then they sat down to collect the good fish in baskets and throw the bad ones away. That is how it will be at the end of time. The angels will come and separate the wicked from the just and throw them into the fiery furnace." (Mt 13:47-50)

Al: In this parable, the net symbolizes the Church that unites in one body all those who follow Jesus. Mind you, there are both saints and sinners in the Church. On the Last Day at the end of time they will be permanently separated either for or against the Lord.

Jo: And you say that Jesus referred to the Church as the kingdom of God on other occasions too?

Al: Many times! And in doing so, he was fulfilling a major prophecy of the Old Testament.

Jo: The Old Testament predicted the kingdom of God?

Al: Yes. For example, take Daniel chapter 7. Here, read it.

Jo: "As I gazed at my visions in the night,
I saw someone, like a son of man,
coming on the clouds of heaven.
He came to the Ancient of Days [God]
and was led into his presence.
He was given authority, glory and kingship.
All peoples, nations, and those of every language serve him.
His supremacy is an eternal supremacy that shall never end,
nor will his kingdom ever be destroyed." (Dan 7:13-14)

Al: Recall that numerous times Jesus referred to himself as "the Son of Man." By the way, the rabbis could never understand why in Daniel's vision, this son of man is coming on the clouds of heaven. Clouds were exclusively God's chariot—and his alone!
     Now then, let's move on:
A *sheepfold* is another image that Jesus used. Here, read this parable, that is recorded in John's gospel: (Jn 10:11-16)

Jo: "I am the good shepherd. The good shepherd—unlike the hired hand—lays down his life for the sheep. I know my sheep and my sheep know me—and I lay down my life for them. I also have other sheep that are not a part of this flock. These I also have to lead, so that there will be only one flock and one shepherd."

Al: Here we have a clear example of Jesus' intention that all of his followers should be gathered in a worldwide group with him as the chief shepherd, leading us. "Pastor" is the Latin word for shepherd. So while we have many local pastors taking care of their congregations, everyone worldwide is to be united as one, under the lordship of Jesus as the Chief Shepherd.

Jo: And how is that supposed to happen?

Al: Jesus not only founded a Church, but he also gave his Church a definite structure with leaders to guide her after he was gone.

Jo: How did you arrive at that conclusion?

Al: From the gospels. Almost all believers admit these basic facts:
- From the start, Jesus selected twelve men to be his close followers. He also named them "apostles." (Mk 3:13-19)
- For three years he instructed them about the basics of the Kingdom—his Church, as it came to be known.
- He gave them authority to judge dissenters and, if they didn't repent, to expel them from the Church. (Mt 18:15-17)
- And after his departure, Jesus would ratify in heaven all the major decisions that the apostles made on earth. (Mt 18:18)
- The Holy Spirit, whom the Father would send in Jesus' name, would remind them of everything that he had taught in order to prevent them from teaching error. (Jn 14:27)

Jo: That's quite a lot to digest. But I still don't see how you prove a *worldwide* church of believers just from those references.

Al: That's a good point. For the answer, let's examine the very end of Matthew's gospel. Here, read it, please.

Jo: Then Jesus came to them [the apostles] and said: "All authority in heaven and on earth has been given to me. Therefore, go and make disciples of all the nations. Baptize them in the name of the Father and of the Son and of the Holy Spirit; and teach them to observe all that I have commanded you. And behold, I am with you always, even to the end of time." (Mt 28:18-20)

Al: There you have it, Jo. Jesus directed the apostles to go and make *all the peoples of the world* his followers. And he promised to be with them until the end of time.

Jo: But they were going to die. So how could they go on teaching in Jesus' name until the end of time?

Al: We already examined that item when we showed how Peter was the leader of the apostles.

Jo: Ah, yes, I recall that now. That's when you explained how the first apostles, before they died, chose successors to replace them. We call them bishops today. And the one who replaces Peter is the bishop of Rome—the Pope.

Al: Good! You remembered. Now let's look at another image used for the Church in the New Testament. Do you know what it is?

Jo: I haven't a clue.

Al: The Bride of Christ.

Jo: The Bride of Christ? But how?

Al: First, let's go to the Old Testament as a backdrop. Do you know what happened on Mt. Sinai?

Jo: Sure. That's where God gave Moses the Ten Commandments after he led the Israelites out of Egypt.

Al: But more importantly, that's where God made a covenant with them—when he wedded Israel to himself as his bride.

Jo: You mean the Israelites thought of themselves as God's bride?

Al: Yes! Once settled in the Holy Land, the prophets kept reminding Israel that every time they worshipped false gods, they were being unfaithful to the Lord. The prophet Ezekiel is noted for condemning Israel as an adulteress. (see Ezekiel chapter 16)

Jo: What's that got to do with the Church as the Bride of Christ?

Al: Just as Israel was God's bride in the Old Testament, the Church is the Bride of Christ in the New. Jesus told several parables about wedding banquets: "The Kingdom of Heaven is like a king who prepared a wedding banquet for his son..." Jo, in these parables, who do you think the king represents?

Jo: Could it be God the Father?

Al: Nice reasoning! And the son in these parables is Jesus, who came to earth to marry his beautiful Bride, the Church.

Jo: That's quite a leap you're making. Is there something explicit in the Bible to illustrate that?

Al: Yes. Let's go to the book of Revelation, chapter 21. John has a vision. As he sees the heavens open, he writes: "I saw the Holy City, the New Jerusalem, coming down out of heaven from God, dressed as beautiful as a bride, prepared to meet her husband."

Jo: That's strange talk. Who or what is this New Jerusalem?

Al: In verse nine, John explains: "One of the seven angels...came and said to me, 'Come, I will show you the wife of the Lamb.' Then he took me away in the Spirit to a very high mountain and showed me the Holy City Jerusalem, coming down out of heaven." He then describes the Church as the New Jerusalem, complete "with the twelve apostles as its foundation stones."

Jo: So you're saying that the New Testament uses the Bride as another image for the Church?

Al: Yes! Capital "L" Lamb is the Lamb of God, namely Jesus. Paul uses the image, too: "Husbands, love your wives just as Christ loved the Church and gave himself up for her." (Eph 5:25)

Jo: I like that. It's a great image for the Church.

Al: It certainly is. I'd like to wrap up our discussion with a verse from the prophet Isaiah. Centuries beforehand, he spoke of the marital relationship that Jesus would have with his Church:

> "As a young man marries a maiden,
> so will your Maker marry you.
> As a bridegroom rejoices over his bride,
> so will your God rejoice over you." (Is 62:5)

The Mystical Body of Christ

Saul was determined to exterminate the Christian vermin that was spreading everywhere. He had just left the court of the high priest with letters for the synagogues in Damascus to arrest all the members of this sect and bring them back to Jerusalem in chains.

Approaching Damascus, he was suddenly thrust to the ground by a blinding light from heaven. Then he heard a voice that said, "Saul, Saul, why are you persecuting me?" Saul asked, "Who are you, sir?" —"I am Jesus, whom you are persecuting," came the answer. "Now get up and go into the city. There you will be told what you must do."

Three days later, Saul the persecutor became Paul the believer, who after being baptized, became the staunchest preacher of the gospel of all time.

In that first encounter with Jesus on the road to Damascus, the seed was planted in St. Paul's heart that was to flourish in his letters as the doctrine of the Mystical Body of Christ. It's one of the most startling images for the Church. Let's examine what it means.

Returning to the encounter, we hear Jesus asking, "Saul, why are you persecuting *me*?" Then responding to Saul's question, "Who are you?" Jesus replied, "I am *Jesus*, whom you are persecuting."

Had I been Saul, I would have objected: "I'm not persecuting *you*. I'm persecuting those pesky *followers* of yours who are destroying the faith of Abraham, Isaac and Jacob."

In this encounter with Saul, Jesus was identifying himself with his followers, as he did in the parable of the Last Judgment in Matthew's gospel, chapter 25. [Make it a point to read that passage.] "I was hungry and you gave *me* food...I was sick and you visited *me*...As long as you did it to the least of my *brethren*, you did it to *me*."

St. Paul was to elaborate the image of the Mystical Body in several of his letters:

- **Rom 12:4-5** "Just as each of us has one body with many parts...so too in Christ, we—who are many—form but one *body*..."
- **Eph 1:22-23** "God has placed all things under [Christ's] feet, and made him, as ruler of all things, the *head* of the Church, which is his *body*..."
- **1 Cor 12:12-13** "For just as the *body* is one though it has many parts, and all the parts of the body, though many, form but one body, so it is with Christ. For in one Spirit we were all baptized into one *body*...and we were all made to drink of the one Spirit."
- **Col 1:18** "Now he is the *head* of the *body*, which is the Church."

How do we become members of Christ's Body—the Church? Through faith and baptism.

That's what St. Paul clearly states in **Galatians 3:26-27**: "You are all children of God through faith in Christ Jesus, for all of you who were baptized into Christ have put on Christ."

To illustrate what St. Paul is saying, let's use an analogy from modern genetics. The science of genetics has proved that every single cell of each living entity has a unique code all its own, known as DNA. A lab analysis of a strand of my hair indicates that it's uniquely mine. If one were to analyze a strand of hair from every human being in the world—all seven billion of them—not one would match my DNA. It identifies me—and me alone.

So when someone comes to know the Lord through faith, and seals that faith in baptism, that person then takes on the spiritual DNA of Jesus himself. And everyone else who so believes and is so baptized, likewise "puts on the Lord Jesus" and acquires the same identical DNA. That's how we all become incorporated into his Mystical Body, the Church. He is our Head, seated at the right of the Father in glory, and we are all members of his Body here on earth.

Therefore, the Church is not an *organization*, but an *organism*, a living, pulsating organism—the Body of Christ, which encompasses all the believers throughout the ages who acknowledge the Lord Jesus as their glorious Head!

12. Sacraments: Channels of God's Life

Lord, give me living water that I may never thirst again

Virginia Broderick

Al: Before we begin today's topic, answer me this question. How would you describe a sunset to someone who was born blind?

Jo: Why, I'd say something like this: Out there on the horizon is a glowing red ball that's tinting some clouds above it with these marvelous hues of orange and purple.

Al: "Red...orange...purple?" Hey, remember, he was born blind.

Jo: Oh, that's right. Well, let's try this: It's like some soft music, gently played on a violin. Or, it's like a smooth velvet cloth.

Al: That's better. Still, would the blind person be justified to say, "Forget it! Sunsets are bogus; I've never experienced one."

Jo: Of course not. His denial won't affect the reality of a sunset.

Al: Exactly! Yet that's how countless people treat matters of the spirit. They conclude it's a make-believe world. They fail to realize that we human beings are creatures of two worlds: material and spiritual—namely, creatures of body and soul.

Jo: So how does all that tie in with today's discussion?

Al: We saw in our last discussion that all Christians form part of Christ's Mystical Body: He is the Head, and we Christians are members of his Body. And just as our *physical* bodies grow and develop through various stages of life, so too does the Church, which is the *Mystical* Body. In fact, Jesus set up seven channels —called sacraments—that transmit his divine life to us.

83

Jo: Sacraments? What's a sacrament?

Al: A sacrament has three components: It must be a sign
- perceptible to our senses (visible, audible)
- established by Christ himself while he was here on earth
- to signify and to infuse the soul with grace

Jo: And what do you mean by grace?

Al: Grace, here, refers to sanctifying grace; that is, an unmerited gift that makes us holy or godlike. In reality, it's a sharing in God's own divine life.[29]

Jo: Sharing in God's life? How is that possible?

Al: Let's use an analogy: Let's say that you have a dog that you're very fond of. But as close as you are, he can't communicate with you. One day a scientist invents a special "human-life" serum and shoots 20 cc's into your pet. Your dog now takes on human traits. Even though he still looks like a dog, he can now converse with you and tell you the kind of day he had at the kennels. That's what grace does for us. It makes us godlike.[30]

Jo: Thanks. That helps. And you were saying that there are seven of these sacraments. Why seven?

Al: As I said a moment ago, just as our physical body goes through various stages of growth and development, so does the soul. There is a special sacrament that corresponds to every stage of our physical development, starting with birth.[31]

Jo: Which sacrament corresponds to birth?

Al: Baptism, or Christening, as it's sometimes called. In John, chapter 3, Jesus told the rabbi Nicodemus that unless a person is born again, he will not see the kingdom of God.

Jo: But if you're already born, how on earth can you be born again?

Al: That's what Nicodemus objected. Jesus went on to clarify, "No one can enter the kingdom of God, unless he is born of water and the Spirit." He was referring to the sacrament of Baptism, which is how our souls are infused with God's life, making us adopted sons and daughters of God, our heavenly Father.

Jo: And you say there are six more sacraments for the life of the soul, that correspond with the stages of our physical life?

Al: Yes. But in the interest of time, I have an outline here that gives a brief overview of all seven sacraments. We'll discuss each one under a separate topic as we continue our sessions. But for the time being, why not just examine this outline:

Physical Body	Mystical Body	Set up by Christ
1. We are born	Baptism	Jn 3:5/Mt 28:19
2. We are nourished	Eucharist	1 Cor 11:27/Jn 6:53
3. We mature	Confirmation	Acts 8:14-17
4. We seek pardon	Penance/Confession	Jn 20:22-23
5. We marry	Matrimony*	1 Cor 7:10
6. We have leaders	Holy Orders	Acts 13:3/2 Tim 1:6
7. We become ill/die	Anointing of the Sick*	Jas 5:14-15

*Note: In the Scripture citations it is strongly implied that these two sacraments were established by Jesus. The early Church Fathers are in agreement.

*   *   *

Q & A on the Sacraments in General

1. **What's the technical definition of a sacrament?**
    A sacrament is an external holy sign, instituted by Christ, to transmit sanctifying grace (divine life) to the soul.

2. **Just why are the sacraments necessary?**
    Unlike the angels—who are pure spirits—we are creatures of body and soul. So in ministering to us, the Lord wanted to address both components of our human nature. The sacraments do so by using material objects (water, bread, wine, oil, etc.) coupled with a vocal prayer to transmit God's life to the soul.

3. **Why are there seven sacraments?**
    The main reason there are seven is that's how many Jesus established. Also, each sacrament corresponds to some important stage of our physical development. Please review the chart above.

85

4. **What is meant by the sacraments of initiation?**
   These are the first three sacraments we should receive to live as adopted sons and daughters of God: Baptism, Confirmation, and the Eucharist. If you were baptized in the Catholic Church as an infant, you did not receive them all on the same day. But if you became a member of the Church as an adult, you did receive them at the same time, usually at the Easter Vigil.

5. **Can all the sacraments be received repeatedly?**
   Three sacraments may be received only once in a lifetime: Baptism, Confirmation, and Holy Orders. These three sacraments imprint an indelible mark on the soul, sealing that person forever. For example, just as someone is biologically a child of his parents, so too, through baptism one is spiritually adopted into God's own family.

6. **If the one who administers a sacrament is guilty of a serious sin, is the sacrament still effective?**
   Provided that the minister of the sacrament intends to do what the Church intends by this sacred rite, yes, the sacrament is effective. Sacraments do not depend on the holiness of the minister, but on the grace of Christ. St. Augustine expressed this point as follows: "If Peter baptizes, it is Jesus who baptizes. And if Judas baptizes, it's still Jesus who baptizes."

13. Baptism: Reborn into God's Family

God - keep us, your children, faithful to our calling

©Virginia Broderick

Jo: So today you're going to explain how we're born again.

Al: That's right. It's what happens in Baptism. But let's set our discussion in the context of what preceded Christian baptism. Shortly before Jesus began his ministry, John the Baptist— to prepare the people to receive Jesus—told them to repent of their sins. He then baptized them in the river Jordan.

Jo: Just a moment. I thought you said it was Jesus who established all the sacraments.

Al: That's right. John's baptism was not a sacrament. It was only an outward expression of the people's inner sorrow for their sins.

Jo: Then when did Jesus set up his sacrament of Baptism?

Al: He did it in stages:
1. Recall our last talk—Jesus explained to Nicodemus that to get into God's kingdom, you had to be born again of water and the Holy Spirit. He was referring to the sacrament of baptism. (Jn 3:5)
2. Then, as he's about to return to his heavenly Father, he tells the apostles to make everyone in the whole world a follower of his—"baptizing them in the name of the Father and of the Son and of the Holy Spirit." (Mt 28:19)

Jo: Did the apostles understand that as a commitment to baptize?

Al: Absolutely!

Jo: Well, I have some friends who say that baptism isn't necessary. They belong to a Christian denomination that says faith is all that matters. Baptism is okay, but it's just symbolic.

Al: I don't see how they can hold that. Why did Jesus *command* his apostles to baptize all new believers? They did so right from the start, and continued to do so throughout the Book of Acts:

1. After Peter preached the good news on Pentecost, the crowd asked, "What are we to do?" Peter replied, "Repent and be baptized every one of you for the forgiveness of your sins." About three thousand people were baptized that day.(Acts 2:38)
2. After Saul was blinded on the road to Damascus, he waited three days until God sent Ananias to him, who said: "Brother Saul, the Lord Jesus...has sent me to you for you to see again and to be filled with the Holy Spirit." Saul got up and was baptized then and there. (Acts 9:17-18)
3. On learning that some people in Ephesus had received the baptism of John, Paul said: "John's baptism was a baptism of repentance. He told them to believe in the one coming after him, namely, Jesus." On hearing this, they were all baptized in the name of Jesus. (Acts 19:1-5)

Jo: I have some other friends who say that for a valid baptism, you have to be immersed in a pool of water.

Al: Well, that's the ideal way, since it symbolizes being buried with Christ and then rising with him to a new life. But one may also be baptized by having water poured over the forehead. In either form of baptism, the one who is baptizing must at the same time say, "I baptize you in the name of the Father and of the Son and of the Holy Spirit."

Jo: Just who can baptize? Anyone?

Al: The usual minister for baptism is a bishop, priest or deacon. But in an emergency—namely in danger of death—anyone can validly baptize. All they have to do is pour the water while pronouncing the formula, "I baptize you in the name of..."

Jo: You know those friends I mentioned? They say you shouldn't baptize babies. You have to be old enough to put your faith in Jesus as your personal Lord and Savior—before your baptism.

Al: That's true if you're being baptized later in life. But all an infant needs is that someone—a parent or guardian, who is a believer —must promise to raise the child as a Christian. There are three things to keep in mind regarding baptizing babies or children:

1. Several times in the Book of Acts, an entire household was baptized together. More than likely, there was a baby or some very small children in those families. (Acts 16:33)
2. In the Old Covenant, the Chosen People had to circumcise all their infant boys eight days after birth. Baptism replaced circumcision as the entry rite for the New Covenant.
3. Also, recall what Jesus said: "Let the little children come to me for the kingdom of God belongs to such as these."

Jo: Now, if I understand you correctly, baptism is necessary to be saved. What about those who die before they're baptized or those who live in a remote tribe and never heard of Jesus?

Al: Well, as Paul told Timothy, "God wants everyone to be saved and to come to the knowledge of the truth." (1Tim 2:4)
The Church holds that there are three types of baptism:
1. Baptism of **water**—which is sacramental baptism.
2. Baptism of **blood**—being killed for your faith in Jesus before you had a chance to receive baptism—i.e., a martyr.
3. Baptism of **desire**—when you're preparing for baptism but die beforehand, let's say in an accident.
4. This also applies to all those in remote tribes, as you said, who never heard the gospel but live good lives according to the natural law written in their hearts—see Romans 2:13-16. This teaching was reinforced at Vatican Council II: "Those who, through no fault of their own, do not know the Gospel of Christ or his Church, but who still seek God with a sincere heart, and—moved by grace—try in their actions to do his will as they know it through the dictates of their conscience—these too may attain eternal salvation."[32]

Jo: Before we conclude, could you summarize for me the major benefits of the sacrament of baptism?

Al: Of course! Through baptism we're blessed in three ways:
1. It counteracts the rebellion that we inherited through the original sin committed by Adam. "Death came through Adam, life came through Jesus Christ!" See Rom 5:15-17. It also forgives personal sins that we have committed.
2. We become members of God's own family, as his adopted sons and daughters. Baptism makes us partakers in the divine nature and living temples of God's Holy Spirit.
3. Baptism makes us members of the Body of Christ—the Church. "For by one Spirit, we were all baptized into one body." (1 Cor 12:13)

Jo: That reminds me. When we discussed the Church a while ago, I asked if everyone was supposed to join the Catholic Church. You said you'd answer that when we discussed baptism. Well?

Al: Thanks for the reminder. All Christians—if properly baptized—by that very fact, are members of the Church. Baptism does not require an ordained minister to be administered.

Jo: So then it doesn't make any difference if you're a Lutheran or a Catholic or a Baptist or whatever...

Al: That's not quite true. Yes, those from other denominations are brothers and sisters in Christ. But since we're not fully united, we call them "Separated Brethren." While we are in agreement about many major points of faith, about many others—sad to say—there are still major differences.

Jo: Well, why can't we just compromise and come together?

Al: Jo, that's easier said than done. So we must continue to pray that one day we may all be one, as the Lord Jesus prayed so earnestly the night before he died: "Father, that they all may be one just as you are in me and I in you. May they all be one in us, so that the world may believe that you sent me." (Jn 17:21)

Developing a Closer Relationship with Jesus
by Joe Difato[33]

> In order to be baptized, it's necessary to believe in the basics of the Christian Faith. For someone baptized as an infant, the parents and godparents must promise to share the faith with their child or godchild. On reaching maturity, it is essential for that cradle Catholic to make a personal commitment to the Lord. From his own experience, Joe Difato explains why this is so essential:

How do we grow into mature Catholics? The process is like what the president of a corporation once said, "The key to running a great company (or having a great relationship with Jesus) is making good decisions."—"How do you do that?" he was asked. He said, "Through experience." When asked, "How do you get experience?" the president said, "By making bad decisions."

The only way we can experience authentic ongoing conversion is by getting what's bad in us out (with grace) while allowing the good gifts we have to increase. We have to see it to deal with it—and the Holy Spirit wants to show us the way. (Jn 16:8-11)

Prior to my conversion, when I went to confession, I used to say, "I cussed a few time, I lied a few times" and that was it. When I experienced the presence of the Lord back in 1971—at my conversion—my eyes were opened. I saw how my sin was rooted in my own self-centeredness—getting my TV, my golf, my football, my food, getting my way, my winning. Even at 18, Jesus showed me how I was completely self-centered—even though, outwardly, I was a good Catholic boy.

Prior to my conversion, going to church once a week was all I did. After conversion, I knew I needed and wanted Jesus every day. Without him was like going without food. I love Jesus. He is the best thing that has ever happened to me. He is a loving, precious God, worthy of our lives!

So try to be as open as you can when you go to the Lord. Ask Jesus to show himself to you in new and deeper ways. Ask him to help you take your gifts to new levels for the sake of the Church—and your loved ones. Ask him to show you how you need to change. He will, if you let him. Try to spend some time with Jesus every day. Listen to what he says. Then, test your behavior—test how you think and act each day—and watch the Holy Spirit help you do a great work of conversion in your life—and maybe even in your parish.

Experimentation in prayer with Jesus will lead to experiences of love, hope, peace, and joy—going to Mass more, reading your Scripture, repenting, serving those in need, and on and on and on. These encounters with Jesus will motivate us to please him more in every way.

* * *

From Playboy Soldier to Soldier of Christ

Charles de Foucauld was born in Strasbourg in 1858 of a military family. It was assumed that Charles would also follow in the footsteps of his forbears.

Orphaned at the age of six, Charles and his sister were raised by their maternal grandfather. Charles made his First Communion at the age of 13, but before graduating from high school he had lost his faith.

Charles was then admitted to Saint-Cyr, the military academy, where he spent more time in frivolities than in preparing for his career. Years later he was to write: "At the age of seventeen, I was all egoism, all vanity, all ungodliness, all desire for evil. I was like a madman."

91

After graduation from the academy, he began a liaison with Mimi, which was to continue during his assignment in Africa where she accompanied him as his "wife." When the truth was discovered, they were both sent back to France.

Three months later, on reading in the newspaper that his former regiment was being attacked in Africa, Charles dismissed Mimi and pleaded with his superiors in Paris to reinstate him to his former rank. Reunited with his regiment, he continued on with them until victory was achieved. On being honorably discharged, he decided to reside in Africa for a while, spending time in the Sahara where he became enamored of the solitude and silence.

Back home in Paris once again, he began to experience a yearning for someone to fill the void in his soul. From time to time, he would murmur this prayer, "My God, if you exist, make your existence known to me!"

Then very early one morning towards the end of October 1886, while he was walking past the Church of Saint Augustine, he darted inside to seek shelter from a sudden downpour. Seated in his confessional, the Abbé Huvelin gestured for Charles to approach him. With Charles standing before him, the abbé told him, "Kneel down and make your peace with God." Charles objected, "Mon Père, I do not believe." To which the abbé insisted: "Make your confession, and you will believe."

It had been over twelve years since Charles had received the sacraments. Kneeling down, he unburdened himself of all the sins of his life. As he stood up again, he was certain that not only had his sins been washed clean in the blood of Jesus, but that he had regained his faith as sure and strong as if he had never lost it.

The abbé inquired, "Are you fasting?" When Charles replied that he was, Abbé Huvelin escorted him to the main altar, where he gave him Holy Communion.

Years later, in his spiritual autobiography Charles wrote: "Once I believed that there was a God, I knew that I could do nothing else but live for him alone. My religious vocation dates from the same hour as my faith."

Ultimately Charles was ordained a priest and than returned to his beloved Africa, where he lived as a hermit in the Sahara. His burning desire was to establish a new religious community, which became a reality years after his death—under the name of the Little Brothers of Jesus.

On December 1, 1916, he was shot to death outside his compound by a band of Bedouin bandits.

He was beatified by Pope Benedict XVI as a martyr in 2005.

14. The Holy Spirit: Fire of Love

Come -
Holy Spirit -
Father of
the poor -
giver of God's gifts -
light of hearts

Virginia Broderick

Al: We've seen how we received God's life in our souls when we were born again in Baptism. Now we're going to see how that divine life develops through the Sacrament of Confirmation.

Jo: Just how does Confirmation do that?

Al: By flooding our souls with the Holy Spirit.

Jo: I thought that the Holy Spirit came to us in Baptism.

Al: He does. But Confirmation gives us the fullness of the Holy Spirit. Before returning to his Father, Jesus promised to send the Holy Spirit to his apostles. Here, read from John's gospel what he told them after the Last Supper:

Jo: "It is better for you that I leave. For unless I go, the Holy Spirit will not come. But if I go, I will send him to you… I have much more to tell you, more than you can take in now. But when the Spirit of truth comes, he will guide you into all truth."(Jn 16:7-13)

Al: Now then, as Jesus was about to ascend into heaven, he once again referred to the coming of the Holy Spirit: "Do not leave Jerusalem, but wait for the gift that my Father promised… You will receive power when the Holy Spirit comes down on you. And you will be my witnesses in Jerusalem, in Judea … and to the very ends of the earth." (Acts 1:4, 8)

Jo: What kind of power was Jesus referring to?

Al: Good question! There is a Greek word for power that means "authority." But the word used here is "dunamin," which gives us the English word, "dynamite." So here it means "strength"—the powerful strength that the apostles will need as they travel the world, witnessing for Jesus even to shedding their blood for him.

Jo: And just when did the Holy Spirit come down on them?

Al: Nine days later, on the feast of Pentecost. While the disciples were praying, he came down on them in the form of tongues of fire, turning those frightened disciples into courageous heroes, who began proclaiming the good news of Jesus to everyone.

Jo: I'm curious. Why were tongues of fire used as the visible symbol for the Holy Spirit coming down on the apostles?

Al: In most cultures fire is often a sign of intense love. The Bible has a verse to that effect, "Love is like a blazing fire, like a mighty flame." (Song 8:6) Recall that while discussing the Trinity, we saw how the Holy Spirit is the love relationship between the Father and the Son. That's why tongues of fire signaled his presence.

Jo: So I guess you could say that Pentecost is when the apostles received the Sacrament of Confirmation.

Al: Yes, they were certainly filled with the power of the Holy Spirit. After hearing Peter proclaiming the good news, 3,000 people accepted Jesus and were baptized.

Jo: And when do we receive Confirmation?

Al: Well, in the Eastern Churches, it's given together with Baptism, usually to infants. But in the Catholic Church, you receive it a number of years after reaching the age of reason.

Jo: Why are there two different customs?

Al: First, Confirmation is closely linked to Baptism. When you're confirmed in the Catholic Church—usually by a bishop—you must first renew the promises that were made at your Baptism. So even in the Catholic ceremony, both sacraments are linked.

Jo: Well, are they two distinct sacraments, or just two stages of one and the same sacrament?

Al: They're two separate sacraments, but connected. To illustrate my point, go to the Book of Acts, chapter 8. The deacon Philip has been preaching the good news to the people of Samaria and many believed and were baptized. Here, you continue reading.

Jo: "When the apostles in Jerusalem heard that the Samaritans had accepted the word of God, they sent Peter and John to them. On arriving, they prayed for them to receive the Holy Spirit, because he had not yet come down on any of them; they had only been baptized in the name of the Lord Jesus. Then Peter and John laid their hands on them and they received the Holy Spirit."

Al: I want to point out that Philip was only a deacon, so he could baptize the new believers but he could not confirm them. That's why Peter and John had to come from Jerusalem to do so. You can see from this passage that Baptism and Confirmation are two distinct sacraments.

The Spirit Gives the Church Life and Unity
by A. M. Henry, O.P.[34]

There is an extremely intimate relation between the Holy Spirit and the Church, which no image...can adequately express. We can say that the Church is constituted effectively by the Spirit. "Where the Church is," says St. Irenaeus, "there also is the Spirit of God; and where the Spirit of God is, there also is the Church and the plenitude of Grace." According to the Apostles Creed, creation is attributed to the Father, the work of redemption to the Son, and the Church to the Holy Spirit: "I believe in the Holy Spirit, the Holy Catholic Church..."

The Messiah came, filled with the Holy Spirit. He laid the foundations of the Church, defined its organization, and instituted the sacraments. Then he sent the Spirit who, like the breath of God causing a commotion among the dry bones in Ezekiel's prophecy, gave life to the institution which Jesus founded. Christ set the structure in place, sent the apostles, and instituted the sacramental signs for imparting the grace of the Spirit.

Then came the Spirit, animating and organizing the institution from within. The Spirit is within the Church; he is her life and unity. And it is in order to communicate this life to her that Christ came and departed: "It is better for you that I should go away; unless I do go, the one who is to befriend you will not come to you." (Jn 16:7)

We note that when the apostles speak in their role as leaders of the Church, it is difficult to distinguish what comes from the Church and what comes from the Spirit. At the conclusion of the first council at Jerusalem they wrote: "It seemed good to the Holy Spirit and to us..." (Acts 15:28) When St. Luke gives the account of the missionary commission of Saul and Barnabas, he writes that the brethren at

Antioch "laid their hands on them, and so took leave of them," and they were "sent on their travels by the Holy Spirit." (Acts 13:3-4)

The Church of the Spirit—the Church to which the Spirit gives life and unity—does not cease to be also the Church of Christ. The work which the Spirit executes is not his own work, an independent and completely autonomous work; it is the work of Christ—who has already fulfilled the work of the Father, taught the Father's doctrine, etc. The Spirit consecrates and sanctifies the apostles of Christ; he not only recalls Christ's teaching but makes it intelligible. "He will remind you of everything I have said to you." (Jn 14:26) He brings about sanctification through the sacraments of Christ.

It is Christ who sends the Holy Spirit, and the latter is, between the resurrection of Christ and his second coming...the representative of Christ. Thus, through the Spirit, the glorious and absent Christ is in the midst of his own, even to the end of time. (Matt 28:20)

The Spirit is Christ's dowry to his Church, the "foretaste" of our heavenly heritage (see 2 Cor 1:22), the mystical ring through which the Church is engaged to her divine Spouse. Note especially that the Spirit is not only the sign of the Covenant, but the very Covenant through which the Church is united to Christ and lives in him, and Christ is united to the Church and lives in her. Without the Spirit, the life of Christ would be that of a mere historical character... Through the Spirit, it is otherwise; Jesus lives among his own. He is really present here below just as he was in his mortal life, although in another manner: he is no longer present in his body, but through his Spirit. By the gift of the Spirit, the Master perpetuates in the heart of the Church a lordly spiritual presence, demanding, exacting, unquenchable, that makes all the faithful the very members of his body.

Prayer to the Holy Spirit by St. Augustine

Breathe in me, O Holy Spirit,
that my thoughts may all be holy.

Act in me, O Holy Spirit,
that my work, too, may be holy.

Draw my heart, O Holy Spirit,
that I love but what is holy.

Strengthen me, O Holy Spirit,
to defend all that is holy.

Guard me, then, O Holy Spirit,
that I always may be holy.

15. The Eucharist: Food for the Beloved

Woodcut by James Reid[35]

Al: We're now going to study the sacrament that's known as the source and summit of our faith.

Jo: Really? Which one is that?

Al: The Eucharist. It's the sacrament that Jesus gave us at the Last Supper, the night before he died. When someone is about to die, he wants to give those he's leaving behind something special so that they'll remember him. Jesus gave them—and all of us—the best gift possible, and that was himself.

Jo: You've lost me. Please explain.

Al: I will. But first, let's go back to the year before the Last Supper. Turn to chapter six of John's Gospel. It's a lengthy chapter with three main parts. We'll study each part in turn.

Jo: Here it is. I remember reading this already—It's where Jesus feeds a crowd of 5,000 by multiplying five small barley loaves.

Al: And in doing so, he bypasses the normal, tedious process that produces bread. Do you know what that process involves?

Jo: Well, you mix flour with water and yeast, set it aside for a few hours while it rises, form the small loaves, set them on a tray, and then bake the whole batch.

Al: Exactly! But in place of all that, with a mere blessing over the the five barley loaves, Jesus produced enough bread to feed a hungry crowd of 5,000 until they were satisfied. But do you know a more important thing he proved by working that miracle?

Jo: No, what was it?

Al: Implicitly, Jesus' action proved a resounding fact: "If I so choose, I can suspend the laws of nature for bread." Now then, Jo, take a moment to read part two of chapter six quietly.

Jo. All right...hmm...hmm... While the crowd disperses, Jesus goes up the mountain, alone... The disciples get into their boat and start crossing the lake. Later that night, while the disciples are struggling against a strong wind, Jesus approaches the boat by walking on the water... Then he joins the terrified disciples in the boat, which at once arrives at the other shore.

Al: A rather strange miracle, don't you think?

Jo: You mean walking on water?

Al: Yes. Every other miracle Jesus worked was either to heal people or to help them in some way. What do think he was trying to prove by walking on the surface of the lake?

Jo: I have no idea.

Al: By suspending the gravitational pull on his body downwards in order to keep his body from sinking, Jesus was implying, "I can suspend the laws of nature for my body."

Jo: But why was that so important?

Al: It's the whole point of the third part of chapter six. In part three, a delegation crosses the lake the next day, and engages in a long discussion with Jesus, trying to get him to be their "Bread King." But Jesus uses the occasion to draw the logical conclusion from the first two parts of chapter six with an awesome promise:
   1. Multiplying the loaves = "I can do what I want with bread."
   2. Walking on water = "I can do what I want with my body."
   3. "Someday, I'll give a bread that will, in fact, be my body."

Jo: Before we go on, Al, let me read part three of chapter six again. Now then, I notice several times, Jesus says, "I am the bread of life." Isn't that expression like a...a...

Al: A figure of speech? A metaphor?

Jo: Yeah, that's it, a metaphor. Jesus sometimes uses them in the gospels: "I am the light of the world." "I am the true vine." That is, he's not speaking literally—just symbolically. So in chapter six, he's not promising to feed us with his actual body.

Al: I might agree with you if there had been no Last Supper.

Jo: And why is that?

Al: In all the metaphors that Jesus used, never once did he reverse the position of the subject and the predicate.

Jo: You'll have to explain that one.

Al: Sure. Jesus said, "I am the light of the world." But he never took an oil lamp in his hand, saying, "This is my body." He also said, "I am the true vine." But he never grasped a cluster of grapes, stating, "This is my blood." He also said, "I am the bread of life." Then a year later at the Last Supper, he took real bread, blessed it, broke it and gave it to his disciples, saying, "Take this, all of you, and of eat it. For this (what's in my hands) is my body."

Jo: So you're saying that "I am the bread of life" is not a metaphor in chapter six.

Al: It is when he first said it. But not after verse 51: "I am the living bread that came down from heaven. Whoever eats this bread will live forever. And the bread that I will give is my own flesh for the life of the world."

Jo: I say it could still be just symbolic.

Al: Not when you consider how he went on to repeat it, adding that we must drink his blood as well. And then he allowed many of his followers to desert him, as they complained, "He's talking utter nonsense. Why pay any attention to him?"

Jo: But at the Last Supper it still looked like bread and wine.

Al: That's true. But let's save that till our next encounter. We'll deal with it then.

The Real Presence

That afternoon at Capernaum, Jesus made an astounding statement: "I am the living bread come down from heaven. Whoever eats this bread will live forever. And the bread that I will give, is my own flesh for the life of the world." (Jn 6:51)

Since then, many have refused to take Jesus at his word. Some have said that the Eucharist only represents him, just as the Stars and Stripes represent our country.

However, someone who burns our country's flag is called to task for desecrating the flag, not our country. But in 1 Corinthians, St. Paul emphatically states: "Whoever eats this bread or drinks of the cup of the Lord unworthily will be guilty of the body and blood of the Lord." (1 Cor 11:27)

Furthermore, if Jesus had meant a mere symbolic eating of his flesh, why did he allow his listeners to take him so literally? Elsewhere in John's Gospel, whenever Jesus' listeners had misunderstood him, the misunderstanding was corrected at once. For example:

1. **John 2**: Jesus told the chief priests—who were standing in the Temple courtyard—"Destroy this temple and in three days I will raise it up." The chief priests thought he meant the Temple of stone. So John, the evangelist, had to clarify that Jesus was referring to the temple of his risen body.

2. **John 3**: Jesus said that you have to be born again in order to enter God's kingdom. Nicodemus concluded that Jesus had in mind a physical rebirth ("Surely, a grown man cannot enter his mother's womb a second time to be born again"). Jesus had to point out that the rebirth he meant was spiritual, not physical.

3. **John 11**: On learning that Lazarus was ill, Jesus said he was going to go and wake him up. When the disciples thought Jesus was referring to natural slumber, he had to specify that he meant the sleep of death: "Lazarus is dead." (Jn 11:14)

But when his listeners at Capernaum objected, "How can this man give us his flesh to eat?" far from correcting any misunderstanding, Jesus went on to reinforce his statement by adding that they had to drink his blood as well—something utterly abhorrent to a devout Jew!

When they refused to accept this "intolerable teaching," Jesus allowed them to walk off and leave him. He did not call them back to restate his message in order to make it acceptable by rationalizing: "You misunderstood me! I only meant a symbolic eating of my flesh."

No—turning to the Twelve, he asked them, "Do you want to leave me, too?" Why was Jesus prepared to risk so much—even the loss of his chosen Twelve? The only possible answer is that the presence he was referring to was not symbolic but real. Recent surveys indicate that many Catholics are entertaining serious doubts about the Real Presence of Jesus in the Eucharist. A thorough examination of the sixth chapter of John leaves no room for doubt that Jesus is really, truly, and substantially present in the Eucharist—the Sacrament of His Love.

* * *

Berengarius, a monk of the eleventh century, was the first to deny that Jesus' presence in the Eucharist was real. He claimed that the bread and wine were mere symbols of the Lord's body and blood. He finally retracted his error while on his knees before Pope Gregory VII, as he made the following profession of faith:

"I, Berengarius,
believe in my heart
and profess with my lips
that the bread and wine on the altar,
through the mystery of the holy prayer
and the words of our Redeemer,
are substantially transformed into the true,
life-giving Flesh and Blood of Jesus Christ.

After the Consecration,
they are the true BODY of Christ,
which was born of the Virgin,
nailed to the cross for the salvation of the world,
and is now seated at the right hand of the Father;
and the true BLOOD of Christ,
which flowed from his side.

They are present,
not merely symbolically
or by reason of their effects, but

in their true and proper nature and substance.
This is my faith,
and thus shall I ever teach hereafter."

16. Does the Mass Undermine Calvary?

Ink Sketch by Kevin Davidson[36]

Jo: Al, I'm surprised to learn that the Catholic Church teaches that the Mass repeats the sacrifice of Jesus' death on Calvary.

Al: Well that's not what the Church teaches. The Church holds that the Mass re-presents, that is, makes present on our altars—in a non-bloody manner—the one and only sacrifice of Calvary.

Jo: But doesn't that go against what it says in Hebrews? "Jesus has no need to offer sacrifices every day, as the other high priests do, first for their own sins and then for the sins of the people. He did this once and for all when he sacrificed himself." (Heb 7:27)

Al: That's true. But let's examine this question in proper order. To do so, let's go back to the Passover meal that God ordered to be celebrated every spring, commemorating the escape of the Hebrew slaves from Egypt. Do know the details of that meal?

Jo: Very few. I do recall that each family had to sacrifice a year old lamb and smear its blood on their door posts.

Al: That's right. They had to eat the lamb with unleavened bread, since they couldn't wait for the dough to rise. The important thing to recall is that the lamb was sacrificed to God, begging him to deliver them from slavery. Now then, let's go to the Last Supper, which was the last Passover meal Jesus had with his disciples.

I want you to read the earliest version, written even before the gospels—in St. Paul's first letter to the Corinthians. You read it.

Jo: "I received from the Lord what I handed on to you: The Lord Jesus, on the night he was betrayed, took bread, and after giving thanks, he broke it and said, 'This is my body which is for you. Do this in remembrance of me.' In the same way, after supper he took the cup, saying, 'This cup is the new covenant in my blood. Do this, whenever you drink it, in remembrance of me.' For whenever you eat this bread and drink this cup, you proclaim the Lord's death until he comes again." (1 Cor 11:23-26)

Al: Before sundown that very day, Jesus would die on the cross. Mind you, the Jewish day begins at sundown, not at midnight or in the morning, but when the sun sets. So on the very day of his death—which was just beginning at sunset on Thursday—Jesus gave us this awesome rite that was to perpetuate his sacrifice on the cross until he returns in glory at the end of time.

Jo: But that was just a memorial meal of his death, not a sacrifice.

Al: Well, listen to what Paul tells the Corinthians in the previous chapter. He was calling some of them to task for participating in sacrifices offered to demons. Listen: "Is not the cup of blessing that we bless a participation in the blood of Christ? And is not the bread that we break a participation in the body of Christ? Consider the Israel of old: Don't those who eat the sacrifices participate in the altar? Am I saying that a sacrifice offered to demons is really something?...No. But pagan sacrifices are offered to demons, not to God...And you cannot drink the cup of the Lord and the cup of demons. You cannot partake in the table of the Lord and the table of demons." (1 Cor 10:16-21)

Jo: I still don't see how that proves that the Mass is a participation in the sacrifice of Jesus on Calvary.

Al: It seems obvious that Paul is comparing the Lord's Supper— what we call the Mass—to the sacrifices that pagans offered to idols. This becomes even more evident when you consider what Paul said at the very end of the narrative of the Last Supper: "For whenever you eat this bread and drink this cup, you proclaim the Lord's *death* until he comes again." (1 Cor 11:26)

Jo: But now that he's risen in glory, Jesus can't die any more. So why do we have to keep proclaiming his death over and over?

Al: Because that's how Jesus wants the believers of all the ages to be joined with him in his great sacrifice of love on Calvary.

The Mass is merely "re-presenting," that is, making present on our altars what took place so many years ago on the cross:

- The *victim* is the same: Jesus!
- The *priest* is the same: Jesus! (At the altar the priest merely lends Jesus his voice, to say, "This is my body...my blood." Mind you, the priest doesn't say, "This is *his* body....)
- The *sacrifice* is one and the same. Only the manner differs:
  —On the Cross, it was offered in a *bloody* manner;
  —On our altars, it's offered in a *non-bloody* manner, through the separate consecration of the bread and wine.

Jo: I still can't make any sense out of all the explanations and examples that you've given.

Al: You're right, Jo. So I'd like to close with a rather down-to-earth example that might clarify the main point I'm trying to make. Through the wonder of television, it's possible to connect millions or even billions of people around the globe with one key event— let's say, the Super Bowl or the World Cup.

Jo: That's right. TV sure is a marvel.

Al: Well, since you like to play soccer, let's say you win the raffle to attend the final game of the next World Cup, all expenses paid.

Jo: Oh, that would be great! If only!

Al: Okay, it's the day of the final game of the World Cup. You're in the Munich stadium, or wherever—along with 150,000 fans from all over the world. And I'm at home, watching the game on TV —with an estimated audience of a billion and a half viewers.

Jo: I'm still with you—but I don't see where this is going.

Al: It's quite simple, really. Modern technology has advanced to the point where it can simultaneously join billions of people from all over the world in a single great event, while it is taking place. What, then, is to prevent almighty God from joining everyone down through the ages—who renew what Jesus did at the Last Supper—to take part in his one great sacrifice of love when he shed his blood for us on the cross?

Jo: But that took place almost two thousand years ago!

Al: True! But each time a priest celebrates Mass, and in Jesus' name prays those awesome words over the bread and wine, it's as if he's turning on a spiritual TV set. At that moment, time and space vanish, and we spiritually join with the heavenly court, which John describes in the Book of Revelation:

"Then I saw a Lamb standing before the throne...a Lamb that appeared to have been slain [= sacrificed]...." (Rev 5:6)

Jo: Could you please tie all this together so I can get the point?

Al: Of course! In John's vision, the Lamb standing before God's throne is Jesus. He's been *sacrificed,* that is, put to death—but now *standing,* meaning that he's risen from the dead.

Let's apply this to our analogy of the World Cup: Those inside the Munich stadium witnessing the actual live game, are like those who stood near the cross watching Jesus die—his mother, the apostle John, Mary Magdalene, and the other women.

Those who observe the game on TV represent all those down through the ages who take part in the sacrifice of Jesus, now made present on our altars, in a non-bloody manner, as the Lamb who was slain—that is, *sacrificed*—yet standing before the throne in heaven—that is, *risen* in glory.

Love Sacrificed

In October 1972, a charter flight was transporting the national rugby team from Uruguay to Chile. While flying over the Andes, it crashed. All forty passengers aboard were presumed to be dead. But 72 days later, sixteen of them emerged alive to tell how they had survived on the snow-capped slope where their plane had crashed. The world was stunned to learn their story. For food, they ate the flesh of their fellow passengers who had died in the crash.

In the sixth chapter of John's gospel, Jesus' listeners are likewise stunned to learn the incredible promise that he made: One day he would give them a special bread to eat—a bread that, in reality, would be his own flesh. Is it any wonder that they objected, "How can this man give us his flesh to eat?"

When did Jesus fulfill the awesome promise that he made in the synagogue at Capernaum? At the Last Supper, when he blessed the bread and wine, saying: "Take, eat. This is my body.... Take, drink. This is the cup of my blood." Why did the Lord Jesus want to give himself to us under the appearances of food and drink?

All living things—plants, animals, and human beings—need food to survive. Furthermore, each species needs its own proper food: cows cannot eat meat; man will starve on hay. So too, the divine life that we received in baptism needs its own proper nourishment to survive—the Eucharist. "Unless you eat the flesh of the Son of Man and drink his blood, you will have no life in you." (Jn 6:53)

For almost 2,000 years the Church has firmly taught that whenever the priest at Mass does what Jesus did at the Last Supper, the bread and wine are changed in *substance* to the Lord's true flesh and blood, even though the *accidentals*—that is, the appearances or properties—of the bread and wine remain. Does this seem incredible? The following illustration might shed some light on this marvel:

You grasp an iron bar. How do you know that it's iron? From its weight, color, and hardness. But in outer space, the bar becomes weightless; and in a blast furnace, it becomes a red-hot liquid. Is it still iron? Yes, of course, for its *substance* remains the same. Only the *accidentals* (weight, color, hardness) have changed.

In the blast furnace of God's love at Mass, the reverse of this takes place. The *accidentals* of the bead and wine stay the same; the *substance*[37] changes into the Lord's own body and blood. This marvelous change the Church calls *transubstantiation*.

The manner Jesus chose to hand down his gift of the Eucharist throughout the ages—the Sacrifice of the Mass—was both prefigured and predicted many centuries beforehand in the Old Testament.

First, it was *prefigured* in the offering which **Melchizedek**, king of Salem, made in thanksgiving for the victory Abraham achieved over the five kings. "He brought out *bread* and *wine,* for he was a priest of God Most High, and he blessed Abraham."[38] (Gen 14:18) It's strange that Melchizedek is said to be a priest of the one true God centuries before God established the Levitical priesthood of the Jews.

Melchizedek is mentioned only one other time in the Hebrew Scriptures, in verse four of Psalm 110. This psalm was written by King David who in the first verse places the Messiah, his descendant, at God's right hand. Then in verse four, God takes an oath regarding the future Messiah:

"The Lord has sworn an oath which he will never take back:
'You are a priest forever in the order of *Melchizedek.*' "

Jesus is the Messiah, and here we see that over 900 years before the Last Supper God took an oath that he would give the Messiah an eternal priesthood in the order of Melchizedek, who had offered *bread and wine*!

Second, and more startlingly, it was predicted by the prophet **Malachi** that the Sacrifice of the Mass would replace the sacrifices offered by the Jewish priests, to whom he directs his message: "I am not pleased with you," says the Lord of Hosts, "and from your hands I will accept no more offerings. But from the rising of the sun even to its setting, my name will be great among the Gentiles. For everywhere a pure sacrifice will be offered to my name, since my name is great among the Gentiles," says the Lord of Hosts. Take note that "a pure sacrifice" in Hebrew refers to a "non-bloody sacrifice"—exactly what the Mass is!

Just what motivated Jesus to give himself to us in such an intimate manner? Love—that was his motivation! Love demands union. The greater the love, the more intimate is the union that's desired. The lover longs to be joined to the beloved—in thought, by letters, emails, phone conversations, physical presence, and ultimately—in spousal love—through the love embrace between husband and wife. So much does Jesus love us that he conceals himself under what looks like bread and wine in order to ravish us in the love embrace of Holy Communion!

I would like to close with this moving insight by **Aemiliana Löhr:**

"But one may ask why this tradition was necessary. Was not Good Friday sufficient without Holy Thursday? Was the sacrifice not sufficient without its mystical continuation? The only answer is that the Lord loved us to the end, as a bridegroom loves. He wished to be entirely united to us, to be wholly one with us. He wanted to give us a share in his death so that we might share in his life as well. So great was his love for our freedom that he would not redeem us against our will, or without our sharing in his redemptive action on our behalf. He wanted a bride, not a slave..."[39]

*   *   *

St. Augustine wrote:

I heard your voice from on high:
    "I am the food of the strong.
    Grow, and you shall feed on me.
    But you shall not change me into you,
    as you do with bodily food.
    Rather, you shall be changed into me."[40]

17. Penance: the Sacrament of Peace

The Prodigal by Gustave Doré

Jo: Al, why does the Church insist that you have to confess your sins to a priest? That seems so arrogant. After all, sin is an offense against God, which only he can forgive.

Al: A good point! But first, let's turn to John 20:21-23 and read it.

Jo: Jesus said: "Peace be with you! As the Father has sent me, I am sending you." Then he breathed on them and said: "Receive the Holy Spirit. If you forgive the sins of others, they are forgiven. If you don't forgive them, they are not forgiven."

Al: Jo, what does that passage mean to you?

Jo: I'm not sure—especially that last part. Because everywhere else Jesus says that if someone harms us and later asks for forgiveness, we have to forgive. As Christians, we have no choice.

Al: That's true. But in this passage, the Church sees the basis for the sacrament of Penance. Mind you, this encounter is the first time that Jesus met with his disciples since he was arrested in the garden and hauled off to his trial. If I had been the Lord, I would never have greeted them with, "Peace be with you!"

Jo: You wouldn't? What would you have said?

Al: Simply this: "Oh, so there you are, Simon Peter! You don't know who I am, do you? And you, Philip, Matthew, James, and the rest of you cowards! Fine friends you turned out to be! Deserting me, just when I needed you most!"

109

Jo: Yeah, you're right. I'd be pretty sore, too

Al: But no! Passing through the locked doors, Jesus simply said, "Peace be with you!" In doing so, he had forgiven them. And he went on to give them the authority to forgive the sins of others.

Jo: There you go again—when only God can forgive us our sins.

Al: That's true. But only God can perform miracles of healing, and only God can reveal the Good News. But just as Jesus shared with his disciples the power to heal the sick and to preach the Good News, so too, he shared with them the awesome power of forgiving the sins of others in his name.

Jo: And you say that he did that on the night of the resurrection?

Al: Yes. Otherwise, there is no way to explain the solemnity of the previous verse, "He breathed on them, saying, "Receive the Holy Spirit." Scripture has just one other instance where God breathes on someone—when he communicated the breath of life to Adam at the dawn of creation. (Gen 2:7)

Jo: But how could the apostles back then, or the priests of today judge if someone is sorry enough to have their sins forgiven?

Al: That's a good question. It's the confessor's duty to decide if the penitent has the sorrow needed for pardon. He must find out what the penitent has done, and whether he's ready to change his behavior—otherwise, there's no forgiveness. The process implies that the penitent must *verbally* confess all *serious* sins.

Jo: I see. But I still don't see why we have to confess something as personal as our sinful behavior to a fellow human being.

Al: There are two points I want to make. The first deals with what's called the Seal of Confession. That means that whatever a penitent has confessed, the priest cannot reveal it to anyone for any reason—even if his own life should be threatened.

Jo: Really? Well, that's good to know.

Al: My second point deals with Step Five of the AA Twelve Step Program. Are you familiar with it?

Jo: Not really.

Al: Step Five states: "Admitted to God, to ourselves, and to one other human being the exact nature of our wrongs." The AA manual clearly states that Step Five is the linchpin of the entire program: "Unless Step Five is fulfilled, sobriety is impossible."

Jo: I still don't see why we can't make our admission of guilt to God directly. Why do we have to bring anyone else into this?

Al: In fact, the AA manual deals with that very point. The response given confronts head-on our habit to rationalize. Here, read it.

Jo: "Somehow, being alone with God doesn't seem as embarrassing as facing up to another person. Until we actually sit down and talk aloud about what we have so long hidden, our willingness to clean house is still largely theoretical." Hmm. They may have a point there. I'll have to give that some serious thought.

Al: And while you're at it, factor into the mix what St. Jerome said back in the fourth century: "How can a sick person expect to be healed, if he is too ashamed to show the doctor his wound?"

Jo: I hadn't looked at it that way. Another good point!

Al: Jo, long before Bill Wilson founded the AA program, Jesus, the divine psychologist, had already given us the means to find real peace in the Sacrament of Penance. He made the forgiveness of of sins dependent on our confession to a fellow-sinner, a priest, about our deep sorrow for having offended God. And God, who is so kind and merciful, is only too eager to forgive us and to welcome us back home, just as he welcomed the prodigal son.

Overwhelmed with God's Peace

God's Boundless Love

Long ago, I heard an evangelical preacher on the radio explaining the passage from Romans 5:6-11. He was showing how human love, at its best, gives costly gifts to people who are worthy of the gift. But regardless of how worthy someone might be, we are rarely willing to die for that person. Sometimes we do, but never for someone who is evil or malicious. For example:

- A soldier will fall on a live grenade to save his buddies— but would he do so to save the life of a *terrorist*?
- A fireman will rescue someone from a blaze set by an arsonist— but would he offer to go to prison for the convicted *arsonist*?
- A parent may give all he owns to ransom his kidnapped child— but would he offer to post bond for the captured *kidnapper*?

Yet that is precisely what makes God's love so unique. As St. Paul expressed it in Romans: "It is not easy to die even for a good person—although for someone really worthy, a man might possibly

111

die. But what proves God's love for us is that Christ died for us *while we were still sinners.*" (Rom 5:7-8)

Love is repaid with love. How can we repay the love that Jesus has for us? By repenting of our sins. And the Lord has made that so easy for us by giving us the sacrament of Penance—which is truly the sacrament of Peace!

It's obvious that God loves us when we've been good: any parent loves a well behaved child. But when we've deliberately rejected God through sin, he loves us even more because we need him more.

Recall the parable of the lost sheep. The shepherd leaves the ninety-nine [good] sheep in the corral, while he goes off in search of the [misbehaving] stray. And on finding it, what does he do? Does he kick it along, shouting, "I'm going to teach you a lesson that you'll never forget!"? Is that what he does? No! He carries it home on his shoulders, comforting it, "You poor thing, I was so worried about you. We're going to have a party when we get back."

Jesus concluded the parable with, "There will be more rejoicing in heaven over one *sinner* who repents, than over ninety-nine *good* persons, who have no need of repentance." (Lk 15:7)

I Confess—"I am what you would call a cradle Catholic, but it didn't mean all that much to me. I was a typical twenty-eight-year-old man. I had built a successful small business that employed five people. Everything seemed to be going along well for me, and I felt as if I had my feet on solid ground.

"Then it happened. A close friend invited me to attend a weekend retreat called Christ Renews His Parish (CHRP). I didn't want to go at all. Everything in me said that it would be a huge waste of time. But my friend wouldn't let up. He kept asking and asking. Finally, I gave in and went with him.

"The CHRP retreat was focused on prayer and adoration, testimonies, and a time for confession. We also celebrated the Eucharist together. We read the Bible. The people leading the retreat were sincere and passionate, and I was enjoying myself. But at the same time, I was also counting down the time when it would end and I could get back home.

"Then, something happened to me. One of the testimonies resonated with my past life, and I felt as if I had to do something about what I was hearing. That evening, there was an opportunity for confession—something I hadn't done in years. What's more, this confession was different. The retreat leaders had handed out a sheet to help us look over our lives so that we could come clean. When my turn came, I was able to confess a few things I had done that I had never spoken about to anyone else. I was also able to let go of some hurts that I had been holding onto.

"That confession changed my life. For the first time in years, I felt truly free. My heart was filled with joy, and I knew God was close to me. I'll never forget what the Holy Spirit did for me during that weekend. My life came to life. I felt like I was 'born again.' "[41]

FORGIVENESS: The Summit of Love

On teaching his disciples the Our Father, Jesus elaborated only one of the petitions—the one on forgiveness: "If you forgive others their offences, your heavenly Father will forgive you. But if you do not forgive others, neither will your Father forgive you your sins." The following example of forgiveness so moved me while serving as a pastor in Baltimore that I recorded it in my journal:

February 5, 1990 Today I buried a saint. Her name was Catherine Wilson. Since I've only been at this parish for a short time, I didn't get to meet her until she was admitted to the hospital in December. As we talked, I learned that although she had undergone surgery for the removal of a malignant tumor, her only concern was to resume her visits to the Veterans Hospital. She informed me that she had volunteered there for over thirty years, and for that had been awarded a bronze plaque for 20,000 volunteer hours! Now at eighty-six, she was ever so eager to return to her "boys," as she called them.

At that point, I remarked, "What fine Catholic parents you must have had, Catherine, to have raised a daughter like you!" She chuckled as she replied, "Father, I'm a convert to the faith, and my mother was quite prejudiced against Catholics." I prompted her, "Quite prejudiced?"

She went on to describe the relationship with her mother. When Catherine graduated from college, the family moved to a new neighborhood. After worshipping for a few weeks at a nearby church where she found the preaching dull, Catherine informed her parents that she was going church-shopping. When she selected the Episcopal Church, her mother remarked, "Well, okay—just so it's not a Catholic Church."

Catherine then recounted how she became very fond of Carl Wilson, a coworker in her office—"Father Victor, he was the finest soul that God ever created. There was just one problem—he was Catholic." They dated secretly, fell in love, and became engaged—an engagement that lasted for years because Catherine did not want to offend her mother. Meanwhile, she herself became a Catholic.

113

When she finally informed her mother that she planned to marry Carl in a Catholic ceremony, her mother gave her three days to vacate the house. Preparing for the move, Catherine went to her hope chest in order to wrap the porcelain set of china that she had purchased over several years—one piece per month. On opening the chest, she found every last piece of china reduced to shards.

Then began a four year odyssey during which Catherine sent her mother a card for Christmas, Mother's Day, and her mother's birthday. Each time, the cards were returned unopened, with the envelope stamped, "Return to sender. Refused by addressee." On the same three yearly occasions Catherine also hand-delivered a gift, which she had to leave on the porch, since her mother would not answer the door.

I interrupted: "Catherine, if your cards were being returned to you unopened, what do you think was happening to your gifts?"—"More than likely, they were being tossed in the trash can, unopened."—"And you still delivered them?"—"Father, my mother may have rejected me, but I wanted her to know that I could never reject her. She was still my mother; and God commanded us, "Honor your father and your mother."

Four long years of being rebuffed, yet she continued to reach out in love. All the while, however, Catherine's father maintained regular contact with her by calling her when she was at work. Then one Sunday afternoon, he arrived unannounced while Carl was playing golf. "Catherine, let's go for a little ride," he said.

It was back to the family home. Because of her hesitation, her father encouraged her, "Come on, let's go inside." Catherine continued: "Once inside the door, I caught the aroma of my favorite meal from childhood—sour beef and dumplings. Mother entered from the kitchen, wrapped her arms around me, and with tears streaming down her face, exclaimed, "Catherine, darling, please forgive me for the terrible way I've been treating you all these years!"

Lord, if either of my parents had treated me the way Catherine was treated, perhaps for one year I might have done what she did—perhaps! I would have reasoned: "Look, I've done my part. My mother's the one at fault! Oh, I'll still pray for her—but why waste more time and money on her?"

Yes, Jesus, today I buried a saint. She learned the lesson that you taught so much better than I—even after all my years as a priest. Turning the other cheek, she repaid rejection with love! Catherine, dear sister, may you now rest in peace!

—*Victor Galeone*

114

18. Marriage: a Union of Life and Love

Lord, prosper the work of our hands

© Virginia Broderick

Jo: So today we're discussing marriage.

Al: That's right. Marriage predates both the State and the Church. It was God who established marriage at the dawn of creation. And he did so for a twofold purpose.

Jo: Really? And what was that?

Al: He designed marriage to communicate both life and love.

Jo: What's your source for that?

Al: The two accounts of creation in Genesis. In the first account in Genesis 1:27, we read: "God created man in his own image and likeness, male and female he created them." The next verse gives first command God ever issued. Suppose you read it.

Jo: God said to them, "Be fruitful, multiply and fill the earth."

Al: So you see that the first purpose God intended for marriage is that it be *life*-giving. Without the love embrace between a man and his wife, all human life on earth would die out. In the next chapter, we learn that the other purpose for marriage is that it be *love*-giving. Again, I'd like you to read it.

Jo: "The Lord God said, 'It is not good for the man to be alone. I will make him a helpmate.'... So the Lord God put the man into a deep sleep. He took one of his ribs and enclosed it in flesh; and from that rib he formed a woman, and brought her to the man."

Al: Yes, God meant husband and wife to be intimate friends, giving each other mutual love and support. And so it is that the twofold purpose of marriage is to communicate both *life* and *love.*

Jo: So the sacrament of marriage was there from the beginning.

Al: No. Jesus raised marriage between two baptized Christians to the level of a sacrament. If neither one, or just one is baptized, it's only a marriage but not a sacrament.

Jo: So with a baptized couple you have the sacrament of marriage.

Al: No. Four more components are necessary for a sacramental marriage: It must be freely-chosen, faithful, fruitful, and forever. Let's examine each one in turn. First, **freely-chosen.** Have you ever heard of a "shotgun wedding?"

Jo: Can't say that I have.

Al: Well some years ago, if a young man got his girlfriend pregnant but didn't want to marry her, if her parents forced him to do so, it was called a "shotgun wedding." So the first requisite for a valid marriage is that both parties must freely give their consent. Now let's discuss the **faithful** part. Any idea what that refers to?

Jo: I think so. When you say that a husband has been unfaithful to his wife, it means he's been cheating on her.

Al: Exactly! So for a valid marriage both parties must promise that they will have intimate relations only with each other—all other parties excluded. Adultery means that one or both have broken their promise. Next, let's move on to the third requirement—**fruitful.** What do you think that means?

Jo: Does that have something to do with having children?

Al: Yes, provided that the wife is of childbearing age and neither one is sterile. So when husband and wife join in the love embrace, they cannot use artificial means to prevent a pregnancy.

Jo: And why not?

Al: Because, as we saw from the start, that's how God designed marriage: It must communicate *life* as well as love.

Jo: Is that what the Church teaches?

Al: Yes, and she's taught it from the very beginning. In 1968 Pope Paul restated it in his Letter, *Humanae Vitae.* Read this section:

Jo: "There is an inseparable link between the two meanings of the marital act: the *love*-giving meaning and the *life*-giving meaning.

This connection was established by God himself, and man is not permitted to break it on his own initiative."[42]

Al: I see that you disagree. Well, consider this: God designed our bodies male and female to communicate both life and love. So every time a husband or his wife thwarts this twofold purpose by using birth control, they're acting out a lie. Through the marital act, their body language is saying, "I'm *all* yours," but the artificial device adds, "...*except* for my *fertility*." So in actual fact, they are lying to each other with their bodies.

Jo: Do you really think their body language is saying all that?

Al: Yes, it does. If you think for a moment, sexual communication uses many of the same terms used in verbal communication:
—intercourse: It's original meaning was "to exchange ideas."
—to know: A euphemism for sexual relations. See Luke 1:34.
—to conceive: "I can't conceive how that happened."

Jo: So what's your point?

Al: Answer me these questions about verbal communication:
1. While listening to her husband,
is it normal for a wife to insert plugs in her ears?
2. While speaking with his wife,
is it normal for a husband to muffle his mouth?

Jo: What weird behavior! Of course not!

Al: Why, then, during sexual communication do we tolerate
1. a wife using a diaphragm or taking the Pill? Or
2. a husband employing a condom?

Jo: Hmm. I never looked at it that way.

Al: Worse still, a vasectomy or a tubal ligation renders the sterility permanent. Other than these two procedures, can you name me one other surgery whose sole purpose is to thwart the main function of a *healthy* part of the human body?

Jo: Hmm....No.....No, I can't think of any.

Al: Besides, if the testes or ovaries aren't diseased, why would we want to nullify their function? Could it be that babies are now considered a disease for which sterilization is a very effective means to immunize oneself?

Jo: You're being very judgmental about the actions of some couples. Furthermore, doesn't the Church teach that we must follow the dictates of our conscience? Don't spouses have that right?

117

Al: Yes, of course—provided that it's a *properly formed* conscience. We must conform our individual conscience to the natural law and the Commandments, just as we have to set our clocks by actual sun time. Otherwise, to conform our behavior to a skewed conscience, is like running our lives by a faulty clock.

Jo: So the Church wants couples to have a dozen kids?

Al: No, the Church says that for sound reasons couples may space their children through Natural Family Planning (NFP).

Jo: That's the old Rhythm Method, isn't it?

Al: Far from it. Couples using NFP abstain during the wife's monthly period for seven to ten days. NFP teaches them how to identify that period accurately. Furthermore, NFP has many benefits:
1. It can postpone a pregnancy as effectively as the Pill, and far better than all the barrier methods.
2. It has no harmful side effects—as in the case of the Pill.[43]
3. NFP couples have a divorce rate of only three percent—compared to 50 percent for all other couples.

Jo: And how does a couple learn that method?

Al: Many parishes offer courses during marriage preparation. Or a couple may even take a course online with the Couple to Couple League at www.ccli.org.

Jo: I'll keep that in mind when I'm getting ready for marriage.

Al: And that brings us to the last requirement: **Forever**. Do you want to give that a shot?

Jo: Could it mean that divorce is ruled out?

Al: Right on! Specifically, divorce with the right to marry someone else. On the wedding day, a couple promises to be faithful "*until death*." If one should die, the other is free to remarry.

Jo: That seems so harsh. Why does the Church insist on that?

Al: Because Jesus did. Actually, Moses allowed only the husband to divorce his wife if he found some "uncleanness' in her. But Jesus revoked that law. Here, read what he says in Mark 10:6-9.

Jo: Jesus replied: "At the beginning of creation, God made them male and female. And so a man leaves his father and mother, joins with his wife, and the two become one flesh. So they are no longer two, but one flesh. So what *God* has joined together, let *no one* ever separate."—I just read it, but I don't see why.

118

Al: The Lord is saying that in a Christian marriage, the couple forms one organic entity, like head and heart—not a mechanical one, like lock and key. So to separate the head or the heart from the human body—unlike removing a key from its lock—causes the organism to die. And that's what divorce does to a marriage. Besides, do you recall what St. Paul told husbands in his Letter to the Ephesians? (Eph 5:25-27)

Jo: Can't say that I do. Tell me, what did he say to them?

Al: Here, let's look it up. "Husbands, love your wives, as Christ loved the Church, and gave himself up for her, that he might sanctify her…that she might be holy and blameless."

Jo: Ah yes! I recall that now. I think you mentioned that while you were speaking of the Church as the Bride of the Lamb.

Al: Just as Jesus would never divorce the Church—even if many of her members were unfaithful to him—so too, married couples cannot divorce—with the right to remarry— since they are to reflect in their own lives the love that Jesus has for his Church.

Alive and Fertile

In 1968 Pope Paul VI issued the Encyclical, *Humanae Vitae,* in which he restated the Church's age-old ban on contraception.

What follows are excerpts from an op-ed piece by Roberta Roane that appeared in the *National Catholic Reporter.*[44]

"Yes, I was alive and fertile in 1968. I was 19 and I knew the Pill was a gift from God and *Humanae Vitae* was a real crock. The Pill was going to eliminate teenage pregnancy, marital disharmony and world population problems…."

After recounting her odyssey of bearing three children while switching from the Pill, to the IUD, to condoms, she continues:

"Finally, my husband and I reached a turning point. At a very low point in our marriage, we met some great people who urged us to really give our lives to the Lord and be chaste in our marriage.

"That blew our minds. We thought it meant 'give up sex.' That's not what it means. It means respecting bodily union as a sacred act. It meant acting like a couple in love, a couple in awe, not a couple of cats in heat. For my husband and me, it meant NFP [Natural Family Planning]…and I won't kid you, it was a difficult discipleship. NFP and a chaste attitude toward sex in marriage opened up a new world for us. It bonded my husband and me in a way that is so deep, so strong, that it's hard to describe. Sometimes it's difficult, but that makes us even closer. We revere each other. And when we do come together, we're like honeymooners.

"Sad to say, I was 35 when I finally realized that the Church was right after all. Not the grab-your-sincerity-and-slide-Church of Charlie Curran, but the real Church, the Church we encountered in the Couple to Couple League, the Catholic Church. The Church is right about contraception (it stinks), right about marriage (it's a sacrament), right about human happiness (it flows—no, it floods when you embrace the will of God). It gave us depth. It opened our hearts to love."

Roberta Roane is echoing what St. Paul wrote many centuries earlier:

"Don't you know that your body is a temple of the Holy Spirit, who is in you, whom you received from God?
You are not your own. You were bought at a great price.
Therefore, glorify God with your body!" (1 Cor 6:19-20)

Crime Escalates as the Family Unit Breaks Down

Shortly before his death in 2012, Chuck Colson, the founder of Prison Fellowship, was interviewed by the Executive Editor of Touchstone Magazine. The following is a short excerpt from that interview. Colson is responding to a question about what lessons he had learned from meeting with thousands of inmates over the years.

"…[T]he chief cause of the increase in prison population—tenfold since I got out of prison [1975]—is the breakdown of the family, the lack of moral training during the morally formative years. So if there is one human need that stands out, out of everything that I have experienced in prison ministry, it is the desperate need for families to stay together and create an environment in which character can be learned and experienced, and virtue can be taught and absorbed.

"Character can't be taught like arithmetic; character has to be learned by example. That's how someone who is in his morally formative years learns—in a family environment. [James Q.] Wilson and [Richard J.] Hernstein say that this lack of moral training within the family is the chief cause of crime. Those formative years are from age five to ten or twelve. After that, you play catch-up."[45]

19. Holy Orders: Servant Leaders

to rank first ~ remain the last and servant of all ~

Virginia Broderick

Al: Today we're going to examine Holy Orders, the sacrament by which men are ordained into Christ's priesthood.

Jo: Pardon—but doesn't St. Peter say somewhere that all Christians who belong to the Lord become part of the priesthood?

Al: Yes, he does in 1 Pet 2:9. In baptism we become members of the "priesthood of the faithful"—since baptism makes us one with Jesus, our great High Priest. But additionally, Jesus set up a special sacrament for the ministerial priesthood.

Jo: For what purpose?

Al: To replace the apostles and the other disciples in celebrating the Eucharist and administering the other sacraments.

Jo: And this is found in Scripture?

Al: Yes, in a rite that is known as "the laying on of hands." St. Paul refers to this by telling Timothy: "I remind you to stir up the gift that God gave you when I laid my hands on you." (2 Tim 1:6) And there are other instances. Read this one from the Book of Acts:

Jo: "One day, while they were worshipping the Lord and fasting, the Holy Spirit said: 'Set apart Barnabas and Saul for the work to which I have called them.' So after fasting and praying, they laid their hands on them and sent them off." (Acts 13:2-3)

Al: Now then, there are three levels or grades in the sacramental or ministerial priesthood:

121

1. **Bishops** can trace their origin back to one of the apostles. They, in turn, can ordain other bishops and priests—a thing which priests cannot do.
2. **Priests** are ordained to help the bishop in serving the local church, by preaching the Gospel, shepherding the faithful, and celebrating the Divine Liturgy (Mass) as well as some of the sacraments.
3. **Deacons** are ordained to assist the bishop and priests in in ministering to the local church—see Acts 6:1-6.

Jo: I have a question. Why is it that priests can't marry?

Al: The practice of not marrying [*celibacy*] for priests and bishops of the Latin Rite, and for bishops of the Eastern Rite can be traced back to the early Church. It's a special way for them to express their deep love for the Lord.

Jo: Does that imply that married couples don't love the Lord?

Al: No! They can and do love the Lord. But look at it this way, Jo. In order to prove that you love someone deeply—you try to give that person the best that you have—just like the young man, proposing to the girl of his dreams, gives her that very special ring. Well, the love embrace between husband and wife is the best gift God has given us on the *natural* level. Marriage is so precious that the Church challenges her priests to dedicate their bodies to God in perfect chastity: "Lord, only you are worthy of this precious gift. Take me. I'm all yours till the day I die."

Jo: You said that this practice can be traced back to the beginning. Could you give me some examples?

Al: I'd be happy to:
1. Jesus was never married.
2. In Matthew 19:12, Jesus invites all those who feel called to remain celibate to do so out of love for God: "And there are eunuchs [celibates] who have made themselves so for the sake of the Kingdom of Heaven. Let the one who can accept this teaching, do so."
3. St. Paul never married. And he wanted many more to follow his example: "I wish everyone could be like me [unmarried]. But all have their own special gifts from God—some [to live] one way; others, another way." (1 Cor 7:7)

Jo: I have another question. Why can't women be ordained priests?

Al: Throughout her 2,000 year history, the Church has followed the Lord's example by calling only men to the priesthood.

Jo: True enough! Well Jesus called only Jews to the priesthood. But didn't the Spirit guide the Church to see that Gentiles could also be Christians? (Acts 10:44-48) Well, why not priests also?

Al: That's right. But in 1994, John Paul II wrote a special Letter, *Ordinatio Sacerdotalis,* in which he stated definitively what the Church has taught from the very beginning:

  1. He was speaking as the *supreme head* of the Church on earth, and as the successor Peter—JP II cites Luke 22:23.
  2. He was deciding "a matter of great importance, a matter that pertains to the Church's divine *constitution* itself."
  3. "I *declare* that the Church has *no authority* whatsoever to confer priestly ordination on women."

Jo: That seems so unfair—and discriminatory against women, too.

Al: At face value, perhaps. But doesn't it also seem discriminatory that in the beehive and the ant colony, the males are all subject to the queen? Why is that? I don't know, nor does a biologist, I'm sure. Ultimately, that's the way the Creator designed these highly structured insect societies. Likewise, the fact that women cannot be ordained priests is because that's the way Jesus designed the priesthood.

Jo: You're probably right. Still, I wonder why he didn't allow women.

Al: You get a different perspective if you frame the question in terms of a sacrament. Since the Eucharist is the peak moment when Jesus gives himself to his Bride, the Church, by uniting himself with her in the profound love embrace of communion—doesn't it make sense that the one who represents Jesus at the altar— namely the priest—interacting with his Bride, the Church, should be male so that the symbol might personify the hidden reality more clearly?[46]

Jo: Thanks. That helps explain this practice a little better.

The Power of Love

"When the Power of Love Overcomes the Love of Power, the World Will Know Peace."[47]

One day, the brothers James and John approached Jesus with a request: "Lord, when you enter your glory, let us sit, one at your right and the other at your left." On hearing this, the other ten apostles became indignant since each one felt that he should be the recipient of that honor. Gathering the Twelve around him, Jesus admonished

123

them: "You know that among the pagans their rulers lord it over them and their high officials make their power felt. That must not happen to you. Instead, whoever wants to be great among you must be your servant, and whoever wants to be first among you must become the slave of all." (Mk 10:42-44)

Christians must not be motivated by power, but by love. Among the final thoughts that Jesus shared the night before he died, far more than any other theme was that of love. "A new commandment I give you: love one another, just as I have loved you." Indeed, love is how his followers are to be identified—it's their ID card, so to speak: "By this all will know that you are my disciples, if you love one another." (Jn 13:34-35)

It is through the power of love that we achieve holiness as individuals and greatness as a society, and not through the radical and unfettered "-isms" of this world. Towards the end of his life, Napoleon remarked: "Alexander, Caesar, Charlemagne and I have founded great empires. But upon what did these creations of our genius depend? Upon power! Jesus alone founded an empire upon love, and to this very day, millions are prepared to die for him."

I want to add a final word on what I believe is at the root of the drive for women's ordination: Power! And in this matter, we priests—and especially we bishops—are to blame. Yes, many of us priests and bishops have failed to reflect the image of Jesus in our lives, "who came not to be served but to serve and to give his life as a ransom for many." Instead, many of us, like James and John, continue seeking positions of ever higher honor and prestige. If we truly reflected the Lord—debasing himself as he washed his disciples' feet—would anyone envy us our position? It's a question of the power of love overcoming the love of power.

Still, there is power that comes from following Jesus as a servant. But it's a power that's spiritual, not material. And one does not need to be an ordained minister to possess it. **Mother Theresa** possessed it, as she led the members of the United Nations in Plenary Session to pray together the Prayer of Francis of Assisi. **Dorothy Day** possessed it as she worked tirelessly for the rights of immigrants and poor workers. **Catherine of Sienna** possessed it, as she confronted Pope Gregory XI to his face, challenging him to return to Rome—which he did. **Joan of Arc** possessed it as she led the French troops in the siege of Orleans. And **Our Lady** possessed it, as she set the wheels of our salvation in motion with her lowly fiat, and even hastened the hour of that salvation when she would not take "No" for an answer to the request that she made at the wedding feast of Cana.

20. Are the Commandments Still Valid?

who
loves
Me
obeys
My
commandments

Virginia Broderick

Jo: Yesterday, I heard this radio preacher say that once you've accepted Jesus as your personal Lord and Savior, you don't have to worry about the commandments anymore. Is that true?

Al: That's not what Jesus said. Do you recall the time a rich young man came up to the Lord and asked what he had to do to enter eternal life? (Mt 19:16-19)

Jo: Vaguely. But I forget what the Lord answered.

Al: Jesus said, "If you want to enter into life, keep the commandments." And then he went on to list a number of them.

Jo: Well, why did the radio preacher make that statement?

Al: I'm not sure. But while we're on the topic, let's talk about why the commandments are so important. Earlier in Matthew's gospel, Jesus stated: "Not everyone who says to me, 'Lord, Lord,' will enter the kingdom of heaven, but only the one who does the will of my heavenly Father." (Mt 7:21) Namely, Jesus doesn't want mere lip service from his followers. He wants us to prove our faith by actions and not just words. See James 2:14-24.

Jo: Are all infractions against the commandments the same?

Al: No, there two types of infractions:
    1) Serious or Mortal sins and
    2) Minor or Venial sins.

Jo: Is that in the Bible?

Al: Yes, in 1 John 5:16—"If someone sees a brother commit a sin that is not a deadly sin [*venial*], he should pray to God to give him life—but he should not pray for someone who commits a deadly sin [*mortal*]."

Jo: When dealing with the Commandments, is there one that's more important than the others?

Al: You're touching a theme that Jesus dealt with when an expert in the Law of Moses once asked him which was the greatest of the commandments. We find his answer in Matthew 22:35-40.

Jo: Here, let me find it. "Jesus said to him, 'The first and greatest commandment is: You shall love the Lord your God with all your heart, with all your soul, and with all your mind. And the second is like it: You shall love your neighbor as yourself. The entire Law and all the prophets depend on these two commandments.'"

Well if all the commandments are contained in just two shorter ones, why bother to keep referring to the traditional ten?

Al: We human beings are masters of justifying our misbehavior. The traditional listing helps to keep us honest. No—we will not discard the full Ten Commandments as God gave them.

Jo: But most of them are so negative. "You shall not; you shall not."

Al: I'm sure you realize that in life-and-death situations, it's the short, negative sign that's more effective: a stark skull on top of two crossed bones versus: "Warning! Grave danger! High voltage tower!" In the negative commandments, God is calling out to us, "Don't even get close!"

Jo: Well, I guess you're right.

Al: God is the One who's right. Tell you what: I'd like you to take this explanation of each of the commandments with you and study them. When we meet the next time, I can clarify whatever questions you might have.

These Rules Lead to Life

1. **I am the Lord your God. You shall have no other gods but me.**
   We may no longer be fabricating actual idols for worship. But anyone or anything that we place ahead of God in our lives we have turned into a false god. God is worthy of our worship, love and obedience. Therefore, we should avoid all:
   —superstitious practices

126

—consulting fortune tellers
—occult practices and games, Ouija boards, tarot cards, etc.
—treating wealth and possessions as our god (See Col 3:5)

2. **You shall not take the name of the Lord your God in vain.**
God's name should be treated with respect. To be avoided are:
—blasphemy by speaking or harboring hateful words or thoughts against God, or Jesus his Son
—breaking promises made in God's name
—lying while under oath, i.e., perjury

3. **Remember to keep the Lord's Day (Sabbath) holy.**
For Christians, Sunday, the first day of the week, has replaced the Sabbath as the special day to honor the Lord.[48] Accordingly, unless prevented by illness, Catholics should attend Mass that day or the Vigil Mass on Saturday evening.
   Also, Christians should refrain from work, business concerns, and unnecessary shopping on Sunday.

4. **Honor your father and your mother.**
—Children should love and respect their parents.
—Parents should provide for their children's material and spiritual needs. "The Lord commanded our ancestors to tell the next generation...so that they would not forget God's deeds, but would keep all his commandments." (Ps 78:4, 5, 7)
—Employees and citizens should fulfill the legitimate requests of their employers and civil authorities.

5. **You shall not kill.**
—To kill someone else, except in self-defense, is forbidden.
—Acts of hatred or inflicting bodily harm are also forbidden.
—Having an abortion or aiding someone to procure an abortion are gravely wrong.
—Euthanasia (mercy killing) is likewise gravely wrong.
—Using illegal drugs is also gravely wrong.

6. **You shall not commit adultery.**
The sixth commandment deals with sex. Sex is sacred. God gave us our sexual faculties to be used by husband and wife in the love embrace to express their mutual love and to help God bring new life to earth. Using sex in any other way is seriously sinful:
—*Adultery*: relations with someone who is not your spouse.
—*Fornication*: sexual relations between two single parties.
—*Masturbation*: impure actions with oneself.
—*Use of Contraceptives*: For an explanation, see page 116 & ff.

—*Pornography*: viewing sexual images for fantasy or self-stimulation.[49]
—*Homosexual activity*: relations with someone of the same sex. A homosexual orientation is not sinful in itself. Those struggling with a same-sex attraction should see Jesus in us, as we treat them with respect and compassion. Every sign of unjust discrimination against them is wrong and must be avoided.

Those with a same-sex orientation, who struggle to remain chaste, may be helped in their efforts through a support group, such as Courage: www.couragerc.net. Phone: (203) 803-1564.

7. **You shall not steal.**
This commandment forbids
—theft, robbery, or failing to return borrowed items
—willfully damaging private or public property
—cheating on time sheets, doing poor work, tax evasion

8. **You shall not bear false witness against your neighbor.**
This commandment forbids:
—*Lying*: telling others what is false in order to deceive them.
—*Rash Judgment*: assuming as true the alleged fault of another.
—*Detraction*: disclosing a person's faults to others without cause.
—*Calumny*: telling lies about others, thus ruining their reputation.

9. **You shall not covet your neighbor's wife.**
This commandment forbids harboring lustful thoughts about another's wife or husband—or even about an unmarried person.
As Jesus said, "Whoever looks at a woman lustfully has already committed adultery with her in his heart." (Mt 5:28)
But one should not confuse a temptation with a lustful desire. If one is being tempted and makes efforts to resist the temptation by praying or putting his mind on something wholesome, no sin has been committed. Indeed, it's an act of virtue!

10. **You shall not covet your neighbor's goods.**
This commandment forbids:
—Avarice and Greed are namely, a passion for riches.
—Envy is sadness at another person's success in acquiring goods, and the keen desire to have them for oneself.
Recall Jesus' words: "Wherever your treasure is, that's where your heart will be, too." (Mt 6:21)

21. Prayer: What Purpose Does It Serve?

The Lord bends close
to hear our prayer

©Virginia Broderick

Al: Tell me, Jo, do you pray on a regular basis?

Jo: When I go to church, and whenever I need to ask God for something. Why do you ask?

Al: Because prayer is absolutely essential in maintaining our relationship with the Lord.

Jo: What are your grounds for saying that?

Al: Sound psychology has shown that for a *relationship* to last, it has to be strengthened by *regular communication*. So a husband and wife who don't regularly spend time with each other in some form of solid communication (Not, "Who's driving junior to his soccer game?") will soon find their relationship deteriorating.

Jo: So you're equating prayer with conversing with God.

Al: Exactly! And just as husbands and wives who rarely engage in a meaningful conversation will certainly wind up in a divorce court, so too, if you pray to God only when you feel like it or are in a jam, that's an indication that God doesn't rate in your life.

Jo: That's a rather stark judgment to make.

Al: Not so! You're using God as a spiritual ATM machine.

Jo: I still disagree.

Al: To prove my point, I quote what I heard a radio preacher say years ago: "Our problem in America today is that we've forgotten how to spell love. How do you spell love? T-I-M-E, that's how.

When you love someone, you want to spend time with that person. The deeper the love, the more time you want to spend together. So if a father gives his son another pretext every week why he can't attend his little league game, he doesn't love that child. If he did, he'd want to spend time with him. So if we spend little or no time with God, that's a sign that we don't love him."

Jo: The fact that I don't pray all day long doesn't mean I hate God.

Al: You may not hate him, but your attitude is one of indifference. Jo, when we were studying the Ten Commandments, do you recall the answer that Jesus gave the master of the Law when he asked which was the greatest commandment?

Jo: Not exactly—it was something about loving God.

Al: Here, let's look at it again in Matthew 22:37-38. Read it, please.

Jo: "Jesus replied: You shall love the Lord your God with all your heart and with all your soul and with all your mind. This is the first and greatest commandment."

Al: Jo, I'd like you to do a short, mental spot-check: Yesterday, how much time did you spend on the phone with your best friend? At the spa? On the Internet? Reading the magazine that came in the mail? Watching TV? Roughly, how much time all together?

Jo: Oh, I'd say about five to six hours.

Al: And how long did you spend in prayer or reading the Bible?

Jo: I'm embarrassed to say. OK, I get the point. You have my word. Starting today, I'm going to try to put God in first place.

Al: The Lord be praised! You made my day, Jo!

Jo: But before we leave the topic of prayer, I have a few questions.

Al: Of course.

Jo: I always thought we're supposed to pray only to God. Why is it that Catholics also pray to the saints? Isn't that wrong?

Al: Not at all. There are a number of times that St. Paul asks others to pray for him:
Col 4:3—"Pray for us so that God may open a door for us...."
2 Thes 3:1—"...pray for us that the Lord's message may spread." Now if St. Paul can ask fellow Christians to pray for him, can't we ask the saints, who have preceded us to heaven, to pray for us? When we pray to the saints, the Church is only encouraging us to ask them to intercede with God on our behalf.

Jo: One last question: In praying the rosary, aren't you disobeying what Jesus said about avoiding repetitive prayer? (Mt 6:7-8)

Al: Good question! First of all, consider the following:

1. In the agony in the garden, Jesus prayed to the Father, saying these same words three times: "So he left them and went away and prayed once more, saying the same thing." (Mt 26:44)

2. In the parable where the Pharisee and the tax collector are praying in the Temple, the Pharisee didn't repeat a single thing. But we're told that the tax collector "kept beating his chest as he prayed, 'Oh God, have mercy on me a sinner.'" In the Greek, the special past tense of the verb indicates a repeated action. Besides, Jesus said that the tax collector went home justified, but not the Pharisee. (Lk 18:13-14)

Jo: Well, then, what did Jesus mean by forbidding repetitive prayer?

Al: He was referring to the repetitive prayer engaged in by the pagans who thought that they could manipulate their gods through some form of mumbo-jumbo.

But as far as the rosary is concerned, it's a beautiful prayer where we meditate on the life, death and resurrection of Jesus against the backdrop of a rhythmic sonata of Hail Mary's. We should pray it slowly and with feeling.

Jo: Do you know what impressed me most about this discussion? When you truly *love* someone, you want to spend a lot of *time* together.

Daily Prayer
from *Rediscover Catholicism* by Matthew Kelly[50]

Many people fail to establish a daily habit of prayer in their lives because they approach it with the wrong expectations. Consciously or subconsciously, most people approach prayer expecting it to be easy. The truth is, prayer is perhaps the most difficult thing we will ever do. From time to time, we may get carried away by a moment of inspiration in our prayer, but for the most part, prayer is hard work—work well worth doing, but hard work nonetheless.

You don't become a great athlete by training only when you feel like it. You don't become a great writer by writing only when you feel inspired to write. The saints did not become such fine ambassadors of God on earth by praying only when they felt like praying. In each case, a daily discipline is required.

Many years ago I saw a violinist interviewed. At the time he was considered one of the best in the world. He explained to the interviewer that he practiced for eight to ten hours a day. The interviewer implied that surely at this stage in his career he could ease up a little with the practice. The violinist smiled and said, "If I miss practice one day and perform the next night, I am the only person who can tell. But I can tell my performance is off. If I missed practice every day for a week and then performed, there would be only a handful of people in any audience who would be able to tell that my performance was off. But if I missed practice for two weeks, or three weeks, almost every person in the audience would be able to tell that I was not performing at my best."

The same is true of prayer. If you neglect prayer for a day, you are probably the only person who can tell. But you can tell. You have less patience and you are less focused. If you neglect prayer for a week, several people around you will notice the change in you. But if you neglect prayer for two or three weeks, almost everyone around you will recognize that you are not at your best.

Prayer is central to the Christian experience. A Christian life is not sustainable without it, because growth in the Christian life is simply not possible without prayer. Growing in character and virtue, learning to hear the voice of God in our lives and walking where he calls us—all require the discipline of prayer. And it is not enough to pray when we feel like it. Prayer requires a daily commitment.

St. Augustine:[51]

> Your prayer is like a conversation with God.
> When you read [the Scriptures], God speaks to you.
> And when you pray, you speak to God.

Untied Shoelaces:[52]

When your shoelaces become untied, you immediately lean down and retie them securely. The untied shoelaces could easily trip you up and cause you to suffer a fall. When you find yourself slipping from your spiritual duties, skipping Mass, neglecting prayer, ignoring the needs of others, etc., you could easily fall or trip into the hands of the evil one. Should you find this happening, it is time to kneel down in prayer and tie the ends of your life securely so that [Jesus] can guide your steps and keep you safe. Better yet, never let yourself become untied in the first place. Stay united with your God who loves you as only God can love.

22. Caesar vs. God

*Give Caesar what belongs to Caesar...
and give God what belongs to God*

Jo: I see where the state legislature is debating a bill to legalize same-sex marriage—which has a lot of people upset.

Al: And rightly so. The state is exceeding the boundaries of its competence. From the beginning, marriage has always been understood to be the permanent union of one man and one woman.

Jo: Well, since the state already regulates marriage by requiring couples to apply for a marriage license, why can't it regulate what constitutes a valid marriage?

Al: Before continuing, let's place this discussion in a larger context. Let's go to the gospel text where the Pharisees asked Jesus if it was all right to pay taxes to Caesar. Here, you read it.

Jo: Then Jesus said to them, "Show me a coin for paying the tax." On being handed a silver coin, Jesus asked, "Whose image is this, and whose name?" They answered, "Caesar's." He said to them, "Then give Caesar what belongs to Caesar, and give God what belongs to God." (Mt 22:18-21)

Al: Jesus is here pointing out that the state does have certain rights in order to govern its citizens. But it has no authority whatsoever to infringe on those rights that citizens have directly from God.

Jo: For example?

Al: For starters, we have what the founders of our republic specified in the Declaration of Independence: "…life, liberty, and the pursuit of happiness…." Then the U.S. Constitution lists a number of others, such as freedom of religion, freedom of speech, and freedom of the press. Some of these rights, such as life, liberty and the pursuit of happiness come to us directly from God.

Jo: Well, thank goodness we don't have to worry about the government depriving us of any of our rights!

Al: We don't? What about the innocent captives from Africa that were bought and sold during the period of slavery in the South?

Jo: Ah, that was an unfortunate exception.

Al: No, there were a number of others, as well. But first, I want to address the point we began with—the state legislature that's debating a bill to legalize same-sex marriage. In this case, the state is not abolishing a right that already exists, but rather fabricating a bogus right that no one can ever have.

Jo: Aren't you being too severe in your assessment?

Al: Not at all. Marriage doesn't come from the state—not even from the church. Marriage was instituted at the very dawn of creation by God himself. I stressed that point when we discussed the sacrament of Marriage. Frankly, I'm quite mystified at how so many intelligent people, including some legislators, are attempting to redefine marriage.

Jo: Really? Why so?

Al: Well, let's put it this way: Say that a college professor wanted to expand the definition of water. So one day he informs his class that in addition to the regular chemical makeup of water, H_2O, he wants to add, "HH" and "OO." Do you think the president of the college would permit him to do that?

Jo: No, I don't think he would.

Al: You bet your life he wouldn't. Try putting out a brush fire with the new "OO water" and you might start a forest fire. Or if you cook your noodles in the new "HH water," you'll have brittle pasta for supper. It's the same with marriage. You cannot call the union of two men or of two women a marriage. Just as God created the chemical composition of water, so too he instituted marriage as the permanent union between one man and one woman:

"Male and female he created them. For this reason a man shall leave his father and mother, join with his wife and the two shall become one flesh. So they are no longer two, but one flesh. Therefore, what *God* has joined together, let *no one* ever separate." (Mt 19:4-6)

Jo: Well let's hope that the full legislature doesn't approve that bill.

Al: Now then, rather than continue enumerating the instances where the state has infringed on the rights which citizens possess from God, I'd like to outline the more egregious examples and forward them to you so that you can study them at your leisure.

Jo: Sounds good to me. I look forward to receiving them.

My Country Right or Wrong

"My Country right or wrong!" was a patriotic cry that was often heard when our nation was facing a trying situation. But is it valid? When my country is right—Yes! But not when my country is wrong! One must never cooperate with evil—either directly or indirectly.

Listed below are a number of instances when our own nation or other nations deliberately stripped innocent people of their rights.

I. African Slavery in the South

After Constantine recognized Christianity as an official religion, slavery in the ancient world gradually disappeared.

With the discovery of the New World, however, the slave trade and enslaving the Indians and Africans was practiced by the Spanish and Portuguese landlords in South America.

In North America, the English colonists first purchased slaves in 1619. Thereafter, slavery flourished on the Southern plantations. Here are some facts about the slave trade in our colonies:

- Slaves increased from 700,000 in 1790 to four million by 1860. Most of the latter were born of slave parents in the South.
- Slaves, captured in Africa by warring tribal chiefs, were sold to ship captains for transfer to the colonies. Many died en route.
- Almost 50 percent of the slaves died from the time of their capture in Africa to their purchase by Southern plantation owners.
- The Dred Scott Decision (1857) – The Supreme Court ruled 7 to 2 that descendants of Africans had no claim to U.S. citizenship or even to their freedom. Since slaves were private property, Congress had no power to revoke a slave owner's rights based on where he lived.

Two Papal documents:[53]
1. Pope Paul III in 1537 decreed that the Indians of the New World and all other peoples—even though they were outside the faith—should not be deprived of their liberty. Rather, they should use their liberty freely and were not to be enslaved.
2. Pope Gregory XVI in 1839 ordered all faithful Christians not to enslave any Indians or Negroes or other peoples in the future. Moreover, present owners of slaves were to grant them their freedom at once without selling them to another party.

II. The Slaughter of European Jews
The campaign against the Jews can be divided into two periods:

1. Period of Harassment from the Nazis' obtaining power in 1933 until the summer of 1941.
   - Jews were gradually eliminated from civil service.
   - Journalists, artists, writers, and musicians could no longer practice their professions.
   - Jewish business owners faced ever increasing heavy taxes.
   - As a result, many Jews chose to migrate to other countries, forfeiting all their property and possessions in Germany.

2. Period of Annihilation from summer of 1941 to the Nazi collapse in 1945. This was conducted in two phases:
   - Phase One began when death squads, manned by SS troops, rounded up the Jews in any given town. The Jews were ordered to gather at a specific point, and from there they were transported by truck to a secluded site away from town, where a mass grave had been dug. The poor unfortunates were made to stand at the edge of the huge pit and shot, row after row. It is estimated that the death squads eliminated around 1,400,000 Jews in this fashion.
   - Phase Two began with the extermination camps, such as Dachau and Auschwitz. The Jews were transported in cattle cars to the camps by rail. On arriving at the camps, the victims were marched to the gas chambers, disguised as shower rooms. Groups of 30 to 40—separated by sex—were made to strip in the antechamber, were given a bar of soap, and then ushered into the "shower room"—complete with shower heads located in the low ceiling. Once the doors were shut, poison gas was pumped through the shower heads, while the victims gasped for air.

All told, under the Nazis some six million Jews were executed—most of whom had no foreknowledge of their impending fate.

With some deep reflection, one realizes that the major crimes of history are committed with the cooperation of the type of citizen usually described as decent and respectable. This was eminently true in the case of the destruction of the European Jews. Raul Hilberg writes: "However one may wish to draw the line of active participation, the machinery of destruction was a remarkable cross-section of the German population. Every profession, every skill, and every social status was represented in it."[54]

Among the few notable exceptions was Franz Jägerstäter, an Austrian peasant farmer, who was beheaded in Berlin in 1943 for refusing to serve in Hitler's army, leaving behind a wife and three small children.

III. Mass Killing of Noncombatants

Obliteration killing of innocent civilian noncombatants was unheard of before both Germany and the Allied powers practiced it in World War II. Bombing purely military targets, like airfields and army camps, at times indirectly killed some innocent civilians. But that is not the point of this discussion. We're referring to the strategy of "saturation" or "obliteration" bombing of noncombatants. Let us consider the more egregious examples in order:

1. Starting in the summer of 1940, German warplanes repeatedly bombed London night after night. Many thousands were killed while tens of thousands were left homeless.
2. British and American planes fire-bombed the city of Hamburg in July and August 1943, killing over 30,000 people and leaving almost a million homeless.
3. In February 1945, Allied bombers reduced the city of Dresden to rubble. This was the war's single most devastating attack on civilians—with at least 135,000 killed.
4. On the night of March 9, 1945, American warplanes dropped incendiary bombs on a 12-square-mile residential area of Tokyo, which caused the flimsy houses to ignite in a massive conflagration. The result was 84,000 dead, 41,000 wounded, and a million left homeless.
5. On August 6 and 9, 1945 atomic bombs were dropped on Hiroshima and Nagasaki respectively. In terms of human lives lost, Dresden and Tokyo each had many more losses than either of the cities destroyed with atomic weapons.

6. Some try to defend the Allies' policy of bombing non-combatants: "We were merely repaying the enemy in kind. After all, they started it." Mahatma Gandhi's response to that line of reasoning was, "An eye for an eye until the whole world is blind."

IV. The War on the Womb

One day we shall be judged by how we treated the weakest among us. Measured by that standard, America fails miserably. For in the Roe v. Wade decision of January 22, 1973, the Supreme Court voted 7 to 2 that women had the legal right to abort their preborn babies.

Now then, let's respond to Natalie, an avid, prochoice advocate:

Natalie: So you want to see Roe v. Wade—the 7-to-2 Supreme Court decision—overturned?

Yes, that's my goal, and that of millions of other Americans. In the past, a few Supreme Court decisions have been reversed, including the nefarious Dred Scott decision—which also was decided by a 7 to 2 margin. That decision denied Blacks their personhood, reducing them to the category of mere property.

Natalie: But this ruling is different. It has given women their full rights to control their own bodies.

I want to make two points:
1. The state does in fact pass laws for the common good on what we may or may not do with our own bodies. For starters, we may not jeopardize the life of another, walk down the street naked, jump in front of a moving car, abuse drugs or drive intoxicated.
2. And more importantly, the fetus in the womb is not a body-part of the woman, like her tonsils. Rather, it is an entirely separate individual, with its own distinct DNA.

Natalie: In Roe v. Wade, the Supreme Court ruled that the fetus cannot be granted the protection of personhood under the 14th Amendment since we can't be sure when human life begins.

That's a question for science to answer, not theology. The most prominent embryology textbook in American medical schools today, *The Developing Human*, gives the answer: "Human development begins at fertilization, when a male sperm unites with a female ovum to produce a single cell, a zygote. This highly specialized, totipotent cell marked the beginning of each of us as a unique individual."

Natalie: I guess you wouldn't permit abortion even for the hard cases like rape, incest or the health of the mother?

A therapeutic abortion is permitted only in the case of saving the life of the mother. States that have passed laws permitting abortion for the health of the mother, have discovered that "health" has been so loosely interpreted as to permit an abortion at any stage for the entire nine months of pregnancy.

Natalie: You come across as heartless. What about the poor women in the inner city who have nowhere to turn to for help?

I'd like to respond to your question by quoting from a letter that Dr. J.C. Willke, MD, a pro-life advocate, received from a mother one day. In her letter she related the experience that her son Robert, a high school senior, had in class. I quote from that mother's letter:[55]

"The teacher began the class by informing the students that a high school girl had become pregnant. The teacher then elaborated on the situation. This girl was from a very poor family, yet had a high IQ and would probably be one of the few in her family to escape poverty. She had already been offered a full scholarship to one of the leading universities in the country.

"Her only living relatives were a full-time working mother and a sickly grandmother. She had no one else to turn to who could help care for her baby. So she would have to quit school to take care of the child herself. She would lose the scholarship if she quit school, and would more than likely follow her family history into poverty.

"The teacher asked, 'What should she do?' Just about everyone in the class gave their opinion—almost all of them agreeing that she should have an abortion and stay in school.

"It was then that my son, Robert, raised his hand to give his opinion. He looked around the classroom for a moment and then said, 'If it were left up to you, I would not be here today. That girl was like my mother. You see, I was adopted. My mom was in a similar situation. But she chose to give me life, and then loved me enough to place me in the loving arms of my adoptive parents.'

"After this statement, the other kids in the class came over and apologized to my son. Many of the girls cried or had tears in their eyes. His story had brought home to them that a fetus is more than just a blob of tissue—it's a real person. Even the teacher then concluded the class by saying that if one looks diligently enough for an alternative, they will undoubtedly find a satisfactory solution."

Natalie: You're hitting me with all this drivel to undermine my pro-choice position. Just stick to the facts, please!

Very well, Natalie. You're asking for facts, and the facts you shall have:

1. We condemn the Nazis for exterminating six million Jews. Yet in our own nation some 56 million preborn babies have been aborted since Roe v. Wade.
2. African-Americans comprise 18 percent of the US population. Why is it then that each year, Blacks account for over 36 percent of all abortions performed in our country?
3. Could it be that Planned Parenthood continues to implement what their founder, Margaret Sanger, expressed in a letter she wrote in 1939 to a Dr. Gamble, "We don't want the word to go out that we want to exterminate the Negro population, and the minister is the man who can straighten out that idea if it ever occurs to any of their more rebellious members."[56]
4. Why is it that 80 percent of Planned Parenthood's clinics are located in Black and Latino neighborhoods?
5. Why does our government make annual grants of $350 million or more to Planned Parenthood? Is this a proper use of our tax money? *Thomas Jefferson* would be appalled: "To compel a man to subsidize with his taxes the propagation of ideas which he disbelieves and abhors is sinful and tyrannical."
6. And finally, I close with a quote from Mother Theresa: "If a mother can kill her own baby, what is left—but for me to kill you and you to kill me?"

Natalie: Say what you want—but abortion is still legal!

That's true, abortion is still legal. And it was also legal to kill:

Jews in Germany

Baby boys in Bethlehem

Christ on Calvary

Please note: My heart goes out to all the women of whatever age, who had an abortion. Many did so unwillingly, only at the insistence of a boyfriend or a parent. Years later, these same women struggle with feelings of guilt and worthlessness.

I suggest that they contact Rachel's Vineyard, a ministry dedicated to helping post-abortive women and men. The father of the child may need healing too. This ministry may be reached at: 1-877-467-3463 (1-877-HOPE4ME) or www.rachelsvineyard.org

---

"America is great because America is good.
But if America ceases to be good, America will cease to be great."
—Alexis de Tocqueville, French commentator on democracy, 1835

23. Death: the Door to Eternity

we shall share his victory
over death

Virginia Broderick

Jo: I read in the paper where one of the states just passed a Death with Dignity bill. Do you have an opinion about that?

Al: I heard about that, too. That's just a polite way of describing physician-assisted suicide or euthanasia. As loyal Christians, we can't support that.

Jo: Not even if someone is in a persistent coma with absolutely no chance of recovery?

Al: God is the author of life from conception to natural death. We have no right to terminate the life of an innocent person who is still alive. Once we start making exceptions, the floodgates will open, and then *we*—not God—will be the masters of life.

Jo: How would you define death?

Al: According to Church teaching, we human beings are made up of two components: a mortal body animated by an immortal soul. Death is the definitive separation of the soul from the body.

Jo: And precisely when does that occur? When the heart stops beating? When no brain waves can be measured? Just when?

Al: There's a twilight zone that makes it difficult to pinpoint the exact moment. Some folks have been revived after being under water for more than twenty minutes.

Jo: What about the people who believe in reincarnation? When we die, can the soul enter another body that's newly conceived?

Al: That's what some Eastern religions believe. But our faith holds that each soul is immortal and will be reunited with its own body at the resurrection of the dead on the last day. We'll talk about that at another time.

Jo: I wonder why we have to die in the first place.

Al: The answer is in the book of Genesis. Recall how our first parents failed the test to prove their love for God by disobeying his command not to eat the fruit of the tree of the knowledge of good and evil. Paul wrote about that in his letter to the Romans: Just as sin entered the world through one man—Adam, and through sin, death; so too life and grace entered the world through the obedience of one man—the Lord Jesus Christ. (See Romans chapters 5 & 6)

Jo: How should we prepare for death?

Al: There's a *remote* as well as an *immediate* preparation for death. The remote preparation is to live each day as if it were the last day of our lives. Namely:
1. Keep the two great commandments:
   —Love God above all else.
   —Love your neighbor as yourself.
2. Treat others as you want to be treated.
3. If you're being tempted to do something seriously wrong, ask yourself, "Would I go through with this activity, if I knew that I'd be dead within an hour?"

Jo: And how do you prepare for death when it's immanent?

Al: Among the seven sacraments that Jesus gave us, one is the sacrament of the Sick. It's given not just at the moment of death, but also when you're seriously ill or about to undergo surgery.

Jo: And you say that Jesus instituted this sacrament?

Al: Yes, James mentions it in his letter. Let me find it. Here, read it.

Jo: "Is anyone sick among you? Let him send for the priests of the Church to pray over him and anoint him with oil in the name of the Lord. And the prayer of faith will save him. The Lord will raise him up. And if he has sinned, he will be forgiven." (Jas 5:14-15)

Al: In former days, you had to be in danger of death to receive this sacrament, so it was called Extreme Unction or the last rites. But after Vatican Council II, the Church reverted to the earlier practice of anointing those who had a serious medical condition.

Town Buries Family Doctor, Giving Friend
by Mark Woods[57]

CALLAHAN, FL (6/27/2004)—Even many of those who knew him—and seemingly everybody in town knew Dr. Victor Peña Sr.—were surprised by the request.

He wanted to be buried in the Callahan Community Cemetery. He put it in his will.

"You know that's the black cemetery?" his three children kept hearing as they worked on honoring his request.

It's not just that no white man had ever been buried there. As best as they could tell, no white man had ever *asked* to be buried there.

"He wanted to be buried there with his patients," said Belkis, one of his two daughters. "He wanted to be there with the poorest of the poor."

The cemetery, south of Florida A1A and across the street from a Winn-Dixie [supermarket], is a small, well-manicured piece of land surrounded by a chain-link fence. It is simple and humble, yet remarkable in its own way.

Just like Dr. Peña.

For 28 years, he was Callahan's family doctor.

Rich families, poor families. People with big homes, people with no homes. They came to a small office tucked in the middle of a strip mall. Just a waiting room, three examining rooms, an X-ray room, and a restroom. No computer, no credit cards, and as it said on the front window, "no appointment necessary."

They came because of the doctor who invariably greeted them by saying, "Hello, my friend."

"I think the friend part meant more than the money part," Willie Blair, 76, said. "That's what's wrong with the world today. People who got it look down on people who don't. He wasn't like that. There won't be another like him. Not on this earth."

The file cabinets in his office are full of charts marked "NC." No charge. Even when he did charge, if someone couldn't pay, he didn't bother collecting. One year, his assistant totaled all that was owed that year. It was thousands of dollars.

More money? For what? His family and friends always laughed about his spending habits, about how he went to Big Lots and bought cheap tennis shoes, about how he got all dressed up for one of his children's wedding, then got in the car and promptly put on one of his dollar-store knit caps. He did have one prized possession. A black Mercedes, 1986, with 362,000 miles.

A teenage boy he had known since the boy was a toddler once vandalized that car. The doctor responded by forgiving the boy. The boy responded by looking for ways to make it up to the doctor. There was a lot of that. When patients couldn't pay, they sometimes brought him a homemade cake or cookies or fresh fruit.

"I think he loved that more than being paid," Belkis said with a laugh.

It reminded him of growing up in the Dominican Republic, the son of a cattleman.

He lived 67 years. He died in his sleep June 4. In the days that followed, a steady stream of people showed up at the office, many overwhelmed not only by his death but by his final request. One of them scribbled a note on a piece of paper taped to the door: "I miss you so much. You was a good man. You help people like me. God bless you."

They buried him in the middle of the Callahan Community Cemetery. A prime spot, right under a big oak tree. And when the casket was lowered into the ground, his friends, his patients, wouldn't let the workers shovel the dirt. They wanted to do it. They took turns. Except for that teenager who once vandalized the Mercedes.

He wouldn't let go of the shovel.

He just kept shoveling and shoveling.

Entry from my journal - Oct. 28, 2009

During the Staff Day of Prayer, Sister Elizabeth Hillmann, RC, the oldest of eleven children, shared an event that happened when she was 18. Her father had gone to see his doctor for the results of a lab analysis of a specimen that was submitted the week before. Their mother allowed the children to stay home from school so that they could pray for a favorable report and be there when their dad came home. Later that morning, he returned, beaming from ear to ear as he announced. "I have some good news!" The kids all jumped for joy as they shouted and clapped.

Then he continued: "Yes, I have very good news. The doctor said my tumor is malignant and inoperable." A stunned silence followed. The older children, realizing what he meant, began to sob uncontrollably. "Dad, you can't be serious! How can that be good news?" He continued, "Oh, yes it is. Let us praise the Lord! He is so good to me! He's going to call me home, and he's given me advance notice, so that I can prepare myself to meet him all the better."

He died within six months.

+ *Victor Galeone*

24. Is Hell Eternal?

THE LORD IS LOVE

THE LORD IS MERCY

Virginia Broderick

Al: So far, Jo, we've covered most of the Church's major teachings. But before continuing, I have a question. If you could change just one Church teaching, which one would it be?

Jo: Frankly, I've never given it a thought. Have you?

Al: Yes, I have. If it were up to me, I'd like the Church to change the teaching about hell. Mind you, there would still be a hell—but not one that lasts forever.

Jo: Do you mean to tell me that hell lasts forever?

Al: Yes—that's what the Church has taught from the beginning.

Jo: That seems so cruel. If God is all-merciful, why would he send someone to hell forever for a sin that was committed in a short period of time?

Al: In fact, God sends no one to hell. We damn ourselves there.

Jo: I refuse to buy that.

Al: Take the case of a teenager who just turned 18 and announces to his parents: "I'm out of here! I'm sick and tired of your stupid rules and curfews. You've seen me for the last time." He packs his bag, joins a gang, and becomes involved in criminal activity. Do those parents still love their son?

Jo: I'm sure they do.

Al: Well, can they force him to stay under their roof?

Jo: No—not since he's come of age.

Al: Well this example highlights the tragedy of hell. Bear in mind:
1. God wants everyone to be saved. (1 Tim 2:4)
2. God gives us sufficient grace to be saved. (2 Cor 12:9)
3. No one is lost except through his own fault. God does not reject the sinner. It's the sinner who rejects God—just like that 18 year old rejecting his parents.

Jo: Well, couldn't God punish sinners just for a certain period of time till they've paid their dues—and then bring them to heaven?

Al: Well actually God does that—but only for those who committed sins of a less serious nature, that is, venial sins. Until they've been fully purified of all attachment to sin, they go to purgatory.

Jo: Purgatory? What's that about?

Al: Purgatory comes from the Latin word "to purify." It's a state where those who die but still need to be purified of less serious sins, undergo a period of cleansing so as to achieve the holiness necessary for heaven.

Jo: Is there a Scripture basis for that?

Al: There are several. I'll cite just one: 1 Corinthians 3:12-15. In this passage, St. Paul describes how we must build our lives on the foundation of the Lord Jesus. On this foundation one can build in gold, silver and jewels—or in wood, hay and straw. Regardless of the material, the work of each builder will be revealed on the day of judgment. It will be revealed with fire, which will test the quality of each person's work. If his work survives the fire, he will get his reward. If it is burnt down, he will suffer loss. He himself will be saved, but only as one who has escaped through fire.

Jo: Getting back to the eternity of hell, I still don't understand why the Church teaches such a harsh doctrine.

Al: It's because Jesus taught it. Hell occurs on the lips of Jesus more than anywhere else in the entire Bible.

Jo: You must mean St. Paul—not Jesus.

Al: St. Paul doesn't mention hell once by name! Several times, he gives a list of serious sins, at the end of which he says, "Those who do these things will not inherit the kingdom of God. (Gal 5:21) Paul refers to hell indirectly once by stating those who disobey the gospel "will be punished eternally and shut out from the Lord's presence when he comes in glory." (2 Thes 1:8-9)

Jo: You say Jesus mentions hell more than anyone else?

Al: That's right—over a dozen times. And he invariably says that it's a state of eternal punishment. For example:
Mt 26:41 – "Depart from me, you who are cursed, into the eternal fire that was prepared for the devil and his angels."
Mk 9:48 – "...better for you to have one eye, than to be thrown into hell with both eyes, where...the fire is never quenched."

Jo: If that's the case, why doesn't God just annihilate the person who is damned, rather than have him tortured in hell forever?

Al: I repeat that God damns no one to hell. It's the sinner who has rejected God—and God respects our free will.
Before concluding, I'd like to highlight the following:

1. The Church has never identified anyone by name who might be in hell—not even Judas or Hitler.
2. St. Thomas Aquinas says that the worst suffering in hell is the realization that through one's *own* fault, the sinner is eternally separated from God—the source of all love and joy.
3. Some of the descriptions of hell may be hyperbole—but their common denominator is that the damned will endure horrific suffering. A medieval mystic, Mechthild of Magdeburg, who had a vision of hell, described it simply as "Eternal hatred."
4. While Jesus gives no indication of how many will be saved, he cautions us to make every effort to enter by the narrow gate: "Enter by the narrow gate, for the road that leads to destruction is wide and many take it. But the gate is narrow and the road is difficult that leads to life, and not that many find it." (Mt 7:13-14)

Near-Death Experience: to Hell and Back

In November 2009, I received the following letter from a widow in the diocese. I wrote to her, requesting permission to use her letter discretely by changing the names of persons and places to conceal her identify as well as that of her deceased husband. She responded, granting the permission.

Dear Bishop Galeone,
I would like to share with you an amazing, if not a miraculous event that my husband experienced in March of 1996. He is deceased now and has been for over 10 years.

In March 1996 my husband suffered a severe heart attack. He was in the Cardiac Care Unit of Baptist Hospital for 3 weeks, during which time his heart stopped 3 or 4 more times. Each time the Code Blue team was able to revive him, but he was in very critical condition.

The fourth time his heart stopped, they had a difficult time reviving him, but the doctor kept on trying, shocking him over and over again —more than they normally would. I don't know exactly how long they worked on him, but it was quite a while. Finally, his heart began to beat again—and a week later he was strong enough to come home!

Once home, the first thing he told me was to never let him sleep in on Sunday mornings. He said he wanted to start going to church with me. Except for weddings or funerals of relatives, he had not been to Mass for over 30 years—not even on Christmas or Easter.

He lived for three more years, and during that time he never once missed Mass. He went to confession every four weeks, received Holy Communion and did everything he could to be a good Christian. I thought it was because he knew he didn't have a long time to live, since his heart was severely damaged because of what he had been through.

Then one day while we were sitting in the T.V. room, he said to me, "Marie, I have something to tell you." I asked him, "What is it, Hon?"

He looked at me and said, "I saw hell. I was there, but I didn't go in." I asked him, "What did it look like? Were there flames of fire, like we imagine hell to be?" He said, "No. It was a blackish, red glow as far as I could see. And there were demons, horrible demons in there, looking at me." He said that the fear he felt at the sight was beyond description.

When his heart stopped for the fourth time in the hospital, he must have died for a while, but God sent him back for a second chance.

He accepted that chance, and I'm sure his soul was saved. His last words on this earth were, "Absolution! Absolution!" He was in a semi-coma at the time.

I'm sure God heard him and forgave him his sins. Yes, miracles still happen—even to ordinary people.

Respectfully yours,

Marie Drake

25. Come, Lord Jesus!

My kingdom does not belong to this world

© Virginia Broderick

Jo: In the Creed it says, "I believe in the resurrection of the dead." Does that mean what I think it says?

Al: It refers to the resurrection of the body on the last day. Namely, at the end of the world when Jesus returns in glory, every human being who existed on earth will rise again, body and soul.

Jo: I find that problematic. Why do we believe that?

Al: Because Jesus taught it. For example: "The hour is coming when all those who are in their graves, will hear the voice of the Son of Man and come forth—those who have done good, will rise to life; and those who have done evil, will rise to judgment." (Jn 5:28-29)

Jo: I find that hard to believe. If you died in infancy, will it be an infant body? Or if in advanced old age, will you have a decrepit, ailing body for all eternity? What sort of body will it be, anyway?

Al: The Corinthians had the same difficulty. St. Paul responded very frankly. To paraphrase: "How foolish! That seed that you plant in the springtime—wrinkled, ugly, seemingly dead—is the very means that several months later gives life to a marvelous bloom under the summer sun. That's how the resurrection of the dead will be. The body is buried corruptible, it's raised incorruptible; it's buried in weakness, it's raised in power, etc. (1 Cor 15:35-44)

Jo: But you haven't said at what stage of life the body will be when it rises—as an infant, or in midlife, or in advanced old age?

149

Al: The Church has said nothing definite regarding that. St. Thomas Aquinas speculates that at the resurrection of the dead, we will all have the body at its prime—around the age of 30.

Jo: I also heard that some Christians believe that when we die, we remain dormant, that is, in a state of unconsciousness until Jesus returns at the end of the world. Is that so?

Al: No, that's not true. At death, Jesus judges each person as either for him or against him. The soul is then assigned to heaven, hell or purgatory. We call this the *Particular Judgment*. Then at the end of the world—the Lord's Second Coming—the body is raised from the dead and reunited with the soul for the general or *Last Judgment*. After that, body and soul share the same fate.

Jo: Regarding the Last Judgment, what's our basis for that?

Al: In the first three gospels at the end of his public ministry, Jesus clearly taught about the Last Judgment. He states that he will come in glory on the clouds of heaven, accompanied by all his angels. St. Paul also teaches it in 1 Thessalonians 4:13-18.

Jo: But exactly when will that occur? How can we prepare for it?

Al: We have no idea when it will occur. Jesus said that he will return like a thief in the night. We're not to be concerned about the last day, because the day we die will be our last day. The best way to prepare is to live each day as if it were the last day of our lives. Like the early Christians, we should pray—
COME, LORD JESUS!

The God of Second Chances

While serving as Bishop of the Diocese of St. Augustine, a person I admired deeply was Dale Recinella. Dale served for twenty years as a volunteer chaplain and for thirteen years as a lay chaplain for Florida's inmates on death row and in solitary confinement. He was also a licensed Florida lawyer for more than thirty years.

While Dale and I were having lunch one day, I asked what had prompted him to give up his lucrative law practice in order to serve as chaplain for the death row inmates. I was deeply moved by his response.

On learning that Dale had a book published in 2011, entitled "Now I Walk on Death Row", I purchased a copy. The linchpin of his entire autobiography is the near-death experience that he recounted to me at lunch that day. I requested and received permission from the publishers to reproduce the pertinent passage below.[58]

The point at which I begin quoting the text finds Dale hospitalized for a life-threatening condition which the medical staff has been unable to diagnose. While Dale's wife, Susan, sits at his bedside, his doctor informs him that all his major organs are shutting down:

"Mr. Recinella, Dale." [The doctor] clears his throat. "It's over. You cannot survive the night. You will not live to see tomorrow morning."

Susan is absolutely rigid, except for the squeezing of her hands wrapped around mine.

"Mr. Recinella, you need to get your affairs in order."

The children have visited in the afternoon. Our pastor comes for the last rites. Before losing consciousness I kiss Susan good-bye. She is crying. She is staying. She will be here through the end.

The fever spikes tremendously high. I cannot keep my eyes open. I want to, but am unable to. My last visual moment is Susan, sitting next to my bed. The fever has its way. My eyes fall closed. All is darkness.

Suddenly, at some point in the night, I find myself standing in the center of a room. It is not my hospital room. It is dark except for the illumination pouring from the person in front of me. I recognize him immediately. It is Jesus. He looks exactly like His picture that hung in my bedroom as a child. He is gazing at me intently, but He is not smiling. He is deeply saddened. There are tears on His face. He is weeping softly.

"Dale." His arms stretch out toward me as His head shakes gently with sorrow and disappointment. "What have you done with My gifts?"

The lawyer in me responds by defensive instinct, "What gifts?"

As He lists my skill set, He does not look angry or perturbed, just sad, very sad. I will not be able to wiggle off this hook. He details every aspect of the intellect, education, upbringing, personality and temperament that is part of my worldly success. I still do not get it. The moment does not feel like a judgment. But every response that comes into my head is defensive. "I have worked hard. I have made sure that my children go to the best schools."...

"We live in a safe neighborhood; my family is safe." There is that sensation again. While my mouth is yet moving, in my thoughts I hear the same code being expressed.

"Our future is financially secure." There it is again, the voice in my head, code for "We have filled our barns and are building bigger ones." Only this time the thought comes with a memory of Jesus' words in Luke 12:16-21 about fools who fill their barns.

151

Finally, His hands drop to His sides. His expression is not one of condemnation. Rather, it is like the look of dismay of a parent who has told their teenager something a thousand times and is beyond the point of belief that the child still has not heard it. He speaks with a pleading that borders on exasperation.

"Dale, what about all My people who are suffering?"

In that moment it is as if a seven-foot-high wave suddenly and unexpectedly breaks over me on an ocean beach. I am not at a beach, and the wave is completely transparent, invisible but tangible. I can feel its substance, and it is acidic—corrosive in the extreme.

Somehow intuitively, I know in the moment that the acid is shame, the shame of the selfishness and narcissism of my life. My family is an excuse for taking care of only me, my ego and my false sense of importance. I struggle against the sense of dissolution penetrating every cell of my being, trying to muster a coherent response.

"Please!" I summon the energy for my last plea as Jesus is still tearfully before me. "Please, I promise you. Give me another chance, and I will do it differently."

That is it. That is all. The wave is gone. He is gone. The room is dark.

It is about six-thirty when I open my eyes the following morning. Susan has been sitting next to my bed all night, waiting for me to die.

"I'm not dead, am I?" My voice betrays surprise at hearing itself again. There is a long moment before she responds.

"Well, you look pretty awful." Susan smiles with the full irony of her very long and rough night. "Obviously, you are not dead." There is another long moment of silence.

"Uh-oh." My sigh bears the full weight of having no clue as to what I have promised Jesus I will do.

There is no more fever. The bacterium is gone. The doctor says it is truly impossible. Three years later the bacteria will be identified as *vibrio vulnificus*, a flesh-eating bacterium that causes deadly food poisoning and wound infections. It is overwhelmingly fatal with external exposure. I swallowed it. [*a spoiled raw oyster, six weeks prior*]

Nonetheless, the second half of my prayer has been answered. I have seen myself, my choices and my life as God sees them.

After Susan and I share with each other our experiences of that night, we look for an answer to the question, "Now what?"

In July 1988 we fly to Steubenville, Ohio, and attend a tent revival. The revival is maxed out, with more than one thousand people in attendance. The summer heat is intense. Susan and I have never attended a revival before. The experience is almost overwhelming.

152

On the second night of the three-day weekend, the leader, speaking from the stage, invites anyone who is so moved to stand and proclaim aloud that Jesus Christ is their Lord and Savior. I am not able to stand up on my own. Susan helps me to my feet. I am half-leaning on her and half-balancing on my cane. With a deep determination that almost throws me off balance, I close my eyes and say aloud what I have never shouted out loud before.

"I accept Jesus Christ as my Lord and Savior!"

In a moment I am seated and Susan is standing. Her words seem to come more easily and sound less forced:

"I accept Jesus Christ as my Lord and Savior."

I cannot believe it....For two upper-crust conservative cradle Roman Catholics, it is a tough step. But the proof of the pudding is in the eating. When we stand up in front of all those people and say, "Jesus Christ is my Lord and Savior," we come away knowing it is true in a different way than we knew it before.

From this point in his autobiography, **Dale Recinella** recounts the strenuous odyssey that ensued after he surrendered his heart to the Lord. As a result, he gave up his successful legal practice in Wall St. finance in order to serve the poor and needy in northeast Florida, as well as the inmates on Florida's death row. You can read the full, captivating account in his book, **Now I Walk on Death Row.**

EPILOGUE

In the Jan/Feb 2012 issue of *Catholic Answers Magazine*, I read the conversion story of Paul Sambursky, who is incarcerated at the North Dakota State Penitentiary for another 20 years. Within two months, we began corresponding. I invited him to write this epilogue as a fitting conclusion to this modest work, *Joyful Good News*.

Like many Americans, I had an excellent education in Catholic schools. Unfortunately, it seems that I was just going through the motions and soon forgot everything I had learned in school.

After high school, I joined the Marine Corps. Following my deployment overseas, I met and fell in love with a raven-haired beauty. Soon afterwards, she wanted to get married; but as a self-described neo-pagan, she refused to do so in a Catholic church. So in 1998 we tied the knot in a Las Vegas wedding "chapel."

I was rapidly drawn into the hedonistic lifestyle that my wife espoused. Life became little more than one unending quest for pleasure without any limits or boundaries. I was worshipping false gods.

As my wife and I grew ever closer, I completely fell away from God and His Church. My apostasy was complete—pornography, debauchery, violence and blasphemy became common. My many sins and crimes began to catch up with me. Fortunately the law intervened and I was imprisoned, but only after many innocent people were hurt.

Once in prison, I discovered a pagan group and joined them. Soon, I was running it. Prison did nothing to straighten me out. Instead, I was becoming more bitter, angry and violent than ever. My hatred was all-consuming. Violent dreams kept me from sleeping for most of the night. It was at this point that my wife and children severed their ties with me.

After a few years behind bars, I began to feel some guilt. I was just starting to comprehend what I had done and what I had lost. I didn't know how to deal with it. For a while, I considered suicide. But then I decided that I might as well die while trying to escape. My attempts failed and I thank God that no one was hurt. I was sent to "The Hole" for three years.

For many months, I was allowed nothing but essentials in my cell. I spent countless hours just staring at the wall, stewing in hatred. At times I would scream at the bars. I felt as if I was losing my mind. One day, after months of isolation, I looked up and was surprised to see a Catholic deacon outside my cell. While chaplains did visit the prison, they had never come down to the isolation cells.

Since the deacon began to check up on me every week, he seemed to be genuinely concerned about my well-being. At one of our visits, he brought up the topic of Fatima to rebut an objection of mine.

I was intrigued. Not remembering too much about Fatima, I asked for every book our library had on the subject. I wanted to prove the good deacon wrong. Instead, what I learned changed my life forever.

As I read about Our Lady of Fatima, I started to see her as a living being. Yes, I knew about her Son, Jesus, but I had never accepted him into my heart.

On the deacon's next visit, I asked him for a rosary and a prayer guide. That night, on my knees I prayed for the first time in twenty years. Even before finishing the first decade, I began to cry like a lost child. I knew exactly what I had to do. I desperately needed to be reconciled with God.

Since I was in isolation, it was difficult to arrange for a priest to visit; but I was finally permitted to meet with one. I was brought to a closet-sized room, and bolted to a metal table for my confession. Trying to recall my many sins and crimes after so many years wasn't easy —but it was liberating. Carrying so much guilt for so long was like a huge millstone around my neck. After my confession, I felt as if a massive weight had been lifted.

As I began my walk with the Lord, all my anger, rage and guilt gradually subsided. I have never felt more at peace—since true peace is found only in Jesus. I have since been released from solitary confinement; and I now look on my prison cell as a monk's cell. I find great solace in the knowledge that even in this prison, the Lord is with me. I am also able to comfort and counsel my fellow inmates and help them to find the light of Christ, too.

When Bishop Victor invited me to write this addition to his book, he included with his request, a draft of chapter six. He also stressed that it contains the most important item of the entire book: Surrendering your heart to the Lord Jesus.

I wonder—have you done so? If not, why the delay? I suspect the reason that the bishop wanted to conclude his book with the tragedy of my life was so that you wouldn't make the same tragic mistakes yourself.

So if you still haven't surrendered your heart to Jesus, go back to page 50 and read that section at the top again. And in praying that prayer that's boxed-in, make it come from the bottom of your heart!

Yes! Accept Jesus into your life—and then walk with him everyday until the day he calls you home!

Endnotes

[1] This part on distinguishing good from evil in order to prove there's a moral law is based on an analogy in a talk by Dr. Ravi Zacharias, www.rzim.org.

[2] Excerpts from "Atheist to Catholic" are reprinted with permission. The full article (3/22/09) is found at www.ncregister.com. The National Catholic Register, a Catholic newspaper in the U.S., is owned by EWTN.

[3] From Atheism in Our Time, by Ignace Lepp, end of chapter one. Lepp ultimately became a Catholic and was ordained a priest.

[4] Man's Search for Meaning, by Viktor E. Frankl, ©1959,1962, 1984, 1992 by Viktor E. Frankl. Reprinted by permission of Beacon Press, Boston.

[5] ibid. p. 147

[6] ibid. p. 143

[7] Natural faith occurs, when the person we believe is human. When God is the one we believe, it is supernatural or divine faith.

[8] Matthew Kelly, The Four Signs of a Dynamic Catholic, pp. 82-86, © 2010, Beacon Publishing. Reprinted with permission.

[9] Excerpts from an address, "Being Human in an Age of Unbelief," delivered at University of Pennsylvania by Archbishop Charles J. Chaput, 11/0 7/11.

[10] "Almah" In Hebrew means simply a young [unmarried] woman. But around 200 BC, when the Hebrew was translated to Greek, it became "parthenos" which can only mean a "physical virgin." Besides, if "almah" is translated as "young woman," what sort of sign is that? But a virgin bearing a child is a unique sign, worthy of the Messiah, who is also "God-with-us." Comment by Dr. Lawrence Feingold, www.hebrewcatholic.org.

[11] From "What Life Means to Einstein: An Interview by George Sylvester Viereck," The Saturday Evening Post, Oct. 26, 1929, p. 17.

[12] Mere Christianity, by C.S. Lewis, p. 41, 1952 by Macmillan Publishing Company, 1960 edition.

[13] Excerpts of interview of Barrie Schwortz, conducted by Andrew Dalton, LC, on www.Zenit.org 3/22/12. Used with permission.

[14] Fathers of the Church Series, vol 73, Washington DC, Catholic University of America Press, 1985, pp. 222-224, reprinted with permission.

[15] Acts 23:6 – Paul said, "I am a Pharisee, the son of a Pharisee. I stand on trial because of my hope in the resurrection of the body from the dead."

[16] Homily on First Corinthians by St. John Chrysostom, PG 61, 34-36.

[17] Pope Francis, The Joy of the Gospel, #1 to 3, Vatican Press, 2013.

[18] Unlike English, in Greek the numeral "one" has a masculine, feminine, and neuter form. But although the Father and Jesus are masculine in the original, "one" is neuter: ἕν—i.e., "one in being / one in essence."

[19] Reprinted with permission of the author, www.crossroadsinitiative.com. A ministry of Crossroads Productions, Inc. 1.800.803.0118

[20] Martin Luther, *Commentary on St. John's Gospel*, ch. 16.

[21] Don Awalt is a permanent deacon, serving in St. Joseph Parish (Cockeysville, MD), dawalt@sjpmd.org.

[22] Sheldon Vanauken, commentary in *Crisis Magazine*, Nov. 1992 issue. www.crisismagazine.com, Used with permission.

[23] St. Irenaeus, *Against Heresies.* III, 3, 2

[24] St. Ambrose, *Commentary on Psalm 36*, No. 40. To identify the Church today, just identify those who accept the authority of Peter's successor.

[25] *Life of Sir Thomas More* by William Roper, excerpts, pp. 52-54. 2003 by www.thomasmorestudies.org/docs/roper.pdf .

[26] Thomas Macaulay, excerpt from *Essays on Ranke's History of the Popes*. Macaulay, a British historian, had a deep-seated bias against Catholics!

[27] Quoted in Biblica, 1930, p. 386. More Tombstones from Tell el Yahoudiah, Tell no. 22 (1922).

[28] Passages from *Mary: The Second Eve*, pp.10-11, & p.19 © 1982 by TAN Books and reprinted with their permission.

[29] In the *Summa*, Thomas Aquinas states, "Grace is a sharing of God's own life in our souls." *Summa Theologiae*, 3:62:2

[30] Bishop Fulton Sheen used this analogy in a TV presentation of the 1950s.

[31] Aquinas, *Summa Theologiae*, 3: q. 65, a. 1: "The life of the spirit bears a certain similarity to the life of the body…"

[32] Vatican II, *Constitution on the Church*, paragraph 16, near the end.

[33] Joe Difato, 2012, Publisher of *The Word Among Us*, www.wau.org.

[34] *The Holy Spirit*, by A.M. Henry, O.P. pp. 97-100, 1960, Hawthorn Books, New York, NY.

[35] *Last Supper* 1930, 1958 by James Reid. *The Life of Christ in Woodcuts,* Republished 2009 by Dover Publications, Mineola, NY, all rights reserved.

[36] *Christ Crucified* by Kevin Davidson, 1986, used with permission.

[37] Here, "substance" doesn't refer to the *chemical* substance of the iron bar or of bread. Rather, it refers to the basic reality of the thing in itself. You might not recognize me if I don a disguise, but I still remain the person I was—my *substance* remains unchanged. (Cardinal Avery Dulles)

[38] "Abram" is used in the original text. His name has not yet been changed to "Abraham"—his more familiar name, which I used in the paraphrase.

[39] Aemiliana Löhr, *The Mass Through the Year*, vol. 2, pp. 28-29 © 1959, Newman Press, Westminster, MD.

[40] St. Augustine, *The Confessions,* Book 7, chapter 10.

[41] Reprinted with permission of *The Word Among Us*, 1715 Guillford Dr. #100 Frederick, MD 21704. Easter 2012, 1-800-775-9673.

[42] Paul VI, *Humanae Vitae,* No. 12

[43] The Pill doubles the risk of heart attack in women (*New England Journal of Medicine*). The Pill increases the risk of breast cancer by 44% (Study conducted by the Mayo Clinic).

[44] Reprinted with permission of *National Catholic Reporter*, 115 E Armour Blvd, Kansas City, MO 64111, www.ncronline.org.

[45] Touchstone, May/June 2012, p. 51, www.touchstonemag.com.

[46] This analogy is a paraphrase from "The priesthood is not just a Job," by Fr. Larry Silva, *New Oxford Review*, Sept. 1995.

[47] Title of a song by Jimi Hendrix, rock star of the 1960s. How sad! Although gifted with so much talent, he died at the age of 29 from a drug overdose.

[48] See Acts 20:7 - Paul in Troas: "On the *first day of the week* we gathered to break bread..." Rev.1:10 - "*On the Lord's Day*, I was in the spirit..." Here, Sunday is called "the Lord's Day."(Domenica, Domingo, Dimanche)

[49] Pornography is very addictive. In a survey, divorce lawyers indicated that pornography is responsible for 58% of their cases. For information in addressing a pornography addiction, visit www.provenmen.org.

[50] Matthew Kelly, *Rediscover Catholicism,* pp. 169-170, New & expanded edition, 2010, Beacon Publishing. Reprinted with permission.

[51] St. Augustine, *Commentary on the Psalms*, 85, 7

[52] Helen M. Ross, *Learn from Me...He speaks, we listen*, p. 140, Mantle Publishing, Clearwater, FL, 2006, reprinted with permission.

[53] Paul III issued *Sublimis Deus* in 1537; Gregory XVI, *In Supremo* in 1839.

[54] Raul Hilberg, *The Destruction of the European Jews* (Chicago, Quadrangle, 1961) p. 649.

[55] Reprinted with permission of Life Issues Institute, Inc., www.lifeissues.org

[56] Margaret Sanger letter to Dr. Clarence Gamble, Dec. 19, 1939. Source: *Sophia Smith Collection,* Smith College, North Hampton, Mass.

[57] Mark Woods, Metro Section, p. 1 *Jacksonville Times-Union*, 6/27/2004, www.jacksonville.com. Reprinted with permission.

[58] Recinella, Dale S., *Now I Walk on Death Row,* Chosen Books, a division of Baker Publishing Group, 2011, Used with permission.

To Order

Visit our Website: www.magnificatpress.com

Tel: 832-368-6464 / 281-446-3133

Email: magnificatpress@gmail.com

Bookstores: Call for Bulk Rates